WORD PROCESSING
SYSTEMS, APPLICATIONS
AND ASSIGNMENTS

By the same author
Keyboarding for Information Processing, British edition

WORD PROCESSING
SYSTEMS, APPLICATIONS
AND ASSIGNMENTS

Joyce Stananought

Principal Lecturer
Department of Business Information Processing
Salford College of Technology

McGRAW-HILL Book Company (UK) Limited

London · New York · St Louis · San Francisco · Auckland · Bogotá
Guatemala · Hamburg · Johannesburg · Lisbon · Madrid
Mexico · Montreal · New Delhi · Panama · Paris · San Juan
São Paulo · Singapore · Sydney · Tokyo · Toronto

Published by
McGRAW-HILL Book Company (UK) Limited
Maidenhead · Berkshire · England

07 084677 4

Copyright © 1984 McGraw-Hill Book Company (UK) Limited. All rights reserved. No part of this publication may be reproduced, stored in a retrieval system, or transmitted, in any form, or by any means, electronic, mechanical, photocopying, recording, or otherwise, without the prior permission of McGraw-Hill Book Company (UK) Limited.

345 AB 8765

Phototypesetting by Parkway Group,
London and Abingdon
Printed and bound in Great Britain by
Anchor Brendon Ltd, Tiptree, Essex

For Carol and Zoë

CONTENTS

Preface	*viii*
Part 1 Introduction	*1*
Section 1 Word processing, people and employment	*2*
Section 2 The word processor	*6*
Section 3 Some types of word processing system	*15*
Section 4 Using a word processing system	*20*
Section 5 What can a word processor do?	*26*
Section 6 Some uses of word processing	*32*
Section 7 Health and safety	*36*
Part 2 Practical Units and Assignments	*39*
Starting up the word processor	*40*
Closing down the system	*40*
Learning to use a word processor	*40*
Working the assignments	*41*
Unit 1 Create a new document	*43*
Set left and right margins	*44*
Top margin	*44*
Word wrap	*44*
File a document	*45*
Unit 2 Printing a document	*49*
Proofreading and proof correction	*49*
Unit 3 Check index	*52*
Recall/edit a document	*52*
Cursor movement	*52*
Insert text	*53*
Delete text	*53*
Unit 4 Change margins	*57*
Change line spacing	*57*
Make a new paragraph	*57*
Run two paragraphs into one	*57*
Unit 5 Justified right margin	*60*
Deleting a document from the file	*60*
Unit 6 Inserting additional rulers in text to change margins and line spacing	*64*
Unit 7 Centring lines of text	*67*
Viewing service codes	*67*
Unit 8 Centring blocks of text	*71*

Unit 9	Review functions	74
	Proofread a document	74
Unit 10	Underlining text	77
	Bold type, or emboldening	78
Unit 11	Remove underlining	81
	Remove bold type	81
	Remove centring	81
Unit 12	Left aligned tab stop	84
	Decimal tab stop	84
	Right aligned tab stop	84
Unit 13	Review of functions	92
	Proofread a document	92
Unit 14	Cut and paste to move text	95
Unit 15	Cut and paste to repeat text	99
	Copying text	100
	The underscore key	100
	Repeat character key	100
Unit 16	Protected space	105
	Printing additional copies	105
Unit 17	Opening or marking a space	108
	Changing the pitch, or size, of type	109
	Changing a printwheel	109
	Changing a ribbon	109
Unit 18	Review of functions	112
	Proofread a document	112
Unit 19	Standard and variable information	115
	Copying a document	115
	Printing on headed paper	116
Unit 20	Searching	119
	Inserting variable details in a standard document	120
Unit 21	Search and replace	123
Unit 22	Review of functions covered in the course	126
	Certificate of Competence in Word Processing	128
	Personal Record Log Sheet	129
	Sample headed paper	130
	Index	131

PREFACE

Word Processing—Systems, Applications and Assignments fills an educational need for actual teaching material, in addition to the provision of theoretical background to word processing.

In the practical section of the book, beginning students are given just enough information to help them start *using* a word processor effectively and efficiently. As the text progresses, more detailed information is introduced to enable students to achieve competence in using a word processor for basic text editing purposes. On this sound basis of knowledge and practical experience students will later be able to build further expertise in more advanced word processing operations and the development of skills in information processing.

The book is designed with a positive approach to the complex and varied field of word processing. The general overall aim is to ensure that students are able to apply their skills in operating one type of word processing equipment to any other system they may meet in their future employment. It is important that students do not develop as 'machine-specific operators'—that is, operators who feel confident only in using the system on which they learnt. Students should be aware that they can easily transfer the operating skills they develop through this text to any word processing system they may meet in their future employment, with the aid of the operating manual and a little guidance specific to the system.

Aims

1. To introduce word processing and word processor operation at a level, and in language, that the student can understand.
2. To familiarise students with technical word processing terms.
3. To develop an awareness of the common features and functions of word processors of all types.
4. To develop a sound knowledge of, and skill in, the basic operating techniques of a word processor.
5. To develop an awareness of the ability of an operator to transfer these basic operating skills to any word processing system.
6. To develop a flexible and adaptable approach to word processing.
7. To provide experience and practice in referring to a system manual, under the teacher's guidance, in order to identify the specific routine to be followed for a particular function.
8. To provide experience in abstracting information and instructions from forms.
9. To develop proofreading skills and techniques.

The students

Word Processing—Systems, Applications and Assignments is intended for all students undertaking secretarial studies and business studies courses who need an understanding of the concepts and some skill in the operation of word processors. The book may be used with equal benefit by students following a course that includes a substantial element of keyboarding/typewriting and word processing, or by those for whom a knowledge of word processing systems and techniques is not a major part of their course. The text will also be of great value to word processing supervisors and training officers in business for use in their own 'in-house' training programmes for word processing operators for their company's system(s).

Students undertaking specialist option modules or subject options related to word and information processing as a part of their course will find this text invaluable in its planned sequence of logical steps taking them through the basic background to word processing and 'hands-on' operation of word processing systems.

The text is designed for those students who have at least a basic keyboarding skill. The first few practical assignments involve a minimum of keying in and therefore provide students with an opportunity to develop their word processing skills at a fairly early stage in a course that also includes keyboarding or typewriting.

This text will also provide an invaluable framework for teachers of word processing in progressing through the manufacturer's manual provided with the system in their own school or college in order to develop a simplified classroom system manual. It will provide a means of identifying the techniques and functions that are most appropriate for school and college students, and the most logical sequence of introduction of word processing operations.

Using the book

Part 1 provides a simple, straightforward background to basic word processing systems and equipment. Review questions are provided at the end of each section, and additional questions and answers may be found in the teacher's manual.

Part 2 introduces students to over 40 basic functions, operations and text editing capabilities of word processors in general, and their own classroom word processor in particular. As each function is introduced, the methods used on different types of word processing system are discussed to develop the student's appreciation of the fact that various word processing systems perform the same basic functions, even if the methods of achieving them are different.

Students, under the guidance of their teachers, are encouraged to identify the steps taken and the key sequences that need to be followed in order to carry out a particular function on their own system. These brief instructions, together with a reference to the page of the system manual on which they are explained more fully, may be written by the student into the workbook to provide a simple guide for future reference.

The 25 practical assignments are based on the work of the fictional company of Zocar Word and Data Processing Limited, providing students with an opportunity to become accustomed to the vocabulary used in the word processing field. The assignments provide a logical and progressive sequence of intensive practice in basic word processing functions. Review assignments are provided whenever a number of basic functions have been covered, to consolidate on the student's learning. These review assignments also provide proofreading practice and involve the use of correction signs to revise the text ready for screen editing.

Instructions for assignments are presented through the medium of Word Processing Request Forms, to introduce the students to the skills of abstracting instructions from a form.

A sample of headed stationery is provided on page 130 and this may be reproduced by teachers so that students may print out assignments on headed paper where appropriate.

Technical terms

Wherever technical terms are introduced, these are explained in the text, and for this reason no 'Glossary of Word Processing Terms' is necessary.

Joyce Stananought

PART 1
INTRODUCTION

SECTION 1   WORD PROCESSING, PEOPLE AND EMPLOYMENT

What is word processing?

What is word processing? One thing is certain: word processing is not just about word processors. It concerns the equipment, of course, but although the machines are important, they still need people to operate them, and working procedures to ensure that they are used efficiently.

There have been many definitions, but it is generally agreed that word processing is the combination of people, procedures and equipment involved in transmitting ideas from one person or organisation to another. Office staff, procedures and equipment are dealt with as a single and controlled system, rather than as separate parts of the company's organisation. Workers, work procedures and equipment are not considered as separate units, but as they relate to the whole office system.

Word processing is only a part of what is known as **information processing**, which refers to the automation and integration of all office equipment, systems and procedures, including computers, facsimile equipment, telex, copiers, etc. Word processing is concerned with information, and with ensuring that information goes to the right person, in the right place, at the right time. It is also concerned with ensuring that information is stored securely, but in such a way that it can be rapidly retrieved when required.

The way in which information is handled is of great importance to a company and can contribute to the success or otherwise of the firm. The efficient management of information is one of the most important responsibilities of the office worker.

Word processing includes all the activities involved in the following 'information cycle'.

Originating information	Composing the ideas and putting them into words, either through handwriting, dictation to a shorthand secretary, or audio-dictation.
Transcribing	Transcription of the manuscript or dictation into a form that is traditionally acceptable in business by keying it in to word processing equipment. Alternatively, it may be keyed in directly by the author.
Processing	Processing of the information as required—sorting, selecting or, for example, using the arithmetical functions of the word processor to perform the calculations necessary to complete an invoice.
Printing	Printing out the information on paper, if required.
Revision	Revision and amendment of the information, where necessary.
Copying and duplicating	Copying and duplicating correspondence, reports and other documents where required, using copying and duplicating equipment.

Mailing or distributing	Mailing or delivering the information by internal mail services, by external postal services or by transmitting the information electronically from one word processor to another.
Receiving information	Receiving information from other individuals, departments or organisations and passing it to the appropriate individual or department for processing or action.
Storing	Storage of the information on magnetic media and, if required, on paper or microfilm.
Retrieval	Retrieval of information, when required, from storage.

In carrying out these tasks, word processors play an important role in the office.

Word processing and office procedures

When word processing equipment is introduced into offices, new systems, methods of working and workflow procedures are required. If the functions listed above are to be carried out in an organised manner, the operation of the office needs to be planned and run so that word processing is integrated with the other equipment and systems in the organisation.

As part of that planning and management process, all the personnel involved in the use of word processing at all levels of the company need to be trained in the various skills required—preparing handwritten drafts, dictating, proofreading and revising typed work. It is just as important to ensure that the executives of a company increase their efficiency as it is to try to increase the productivity of secretaries, typists and word processing operators.

Training is needed for the **users** of word processing so that they are aware of what word processors can and cannot do. People who draft out the documents that will be typed in to a word processor may be called **users, authors, originators, principals** or similar names. **User manuals** are often prepared by the management so that authors of documents know what procedures to follow, particularly if a word processing centre has been set up in the company. Rules are usually laid down concerning what kind of documents may be submitted for word processing and the way in which they should be submitted (i.e. manuscript or audio-dictation). The user manual may also include standard layouts of documents (housestyle), details of who is responsible for proofreading documents, the priority system for completion of work, the length of time documents will be stored and retained on disk, the hours of operation of the centre, and so on.

How are word processors used?

Some companies centralise word processing into a word processing centre under the control of a word processing supervisor. Others provide word processing facilities within departments. In some companies a word processor is provided to be shared between a group of secretaries on what is called a **walk-up** basis, which means that they use the equipment when they need it and when it is available. Another approach has been to provide word processors on a walk-up basis for the authors of documents, so that they can key in directly the draft of a document which can later be edited and 'tidied up' by a word processing operator.

Where a word processing centre is operated in a company, it is likely that certain employees will become **dedicated** word processing operators, and the major part of their job will be concerned with using word processors. Other companies prefer a number of people to be proficient in the operation of the word processor, so that staff may be involved in various types of office work during the day in addition to word processing. This approach ensures that there is someone available to operate the equipment when people are sick, or at holiday times. In addition, there is the **casual user** of word processing, who may only need to use the equipment occasionally.

Because the equipment is fairly costly to install, word processing staff are sometimes encouraged to operate on flexible working hours or shift working to ensure the most productive use of word processing equipment. This is one example of a change in office procedures that may be necessary in an organisation when word processing is introduced. One or two companies have even experimented with the idea of working at home, for members of staff whose actual physical presence in the office is not essential.

What makes a good word processing operator?

A good deal of attention has been paid to the selection of staff for word processor operation. Some studies are now being made to try to identify the qualities required in a good operator, but the majority of the information available so far is based on experience.

Several main characteristics, in addition to the usual personal characteristics and qualities looked for in an office worker, have been suggested as important for a word processing operator. These are listed below.

Typing and audio-typing Fast, accurate typing, with audio skills. The speed at which an operator can type in text is important. Typewriting accuracy is also still important, in spite of the fact that corrections are quickly and easily made with the word processing equipment. However simple it is to make corrections, they still take time—whether they are corrected immediately or at a later stage—and therefore mistakes cost money. Audio-dictation is favoured by many companies for the submission of work to the operator, and audio-typing is a useful additional skill.

English Good skills in English—spelling, grammar and punctuation. Some word processors are provided with spelling check functions, but this does not mean that the operator need not be able to spell, because spelling checks have limitations.

Proofreading Accurate proofreading skills. The operator should be capable of proofreading work with speed and accuracy, and able to find and make corrections to errors rapidly and efficiently.

Logical thinking The ability to follow the logic of the word processing system. The operating methods of word processors are structured in a logical and methodical way. The person who is able to approach learning and problem solving in an analytical way will tend to learn more quickly.

Problem solving	An operator with the ability to solve problems is likely to be able to sort out any operating problems that may arise when the equipment is being used. Such an operator may also be able to find, without instruction, new applications of the word processor to the company's work.
Interest and enthusiasm	An interest in, and enthusiasm for, information technology. People who succeed as operators are often those who are able to understand and enjoy working with equipment.
Teamwork	The word processing operator should be able to cooperate with colleagues, senior personnel and authors, be able to understand their requirements, and explain what the equipment can—and cannot—do.
Flexibility	Word processing equipment, and the applications for which it can be used, are developing and changing rapidly. It is important that operators are progressive and flexible in their approach to work.
Background knowledge	An understanding of the various types of information, data, equipment and procedures in a modern business is needed to provide a sound background knowledge of office work and information processing.

Review questions

1. Briefly define 'word processing'.
2. List the 10 activities, any or all of which may be involved in the word processing 'information cycle'.
3. Identify the main characteristics and skills required for a word processing operator.

Activity

Over the period of your course, draw up (with guidance from your teacher) a short user manual for your word processing centre at Zocar Word and Data Processing Limited.

SECTION 2 THE WORD PROCESSOR

As suggested in Section 1, word processing is more than a 'word processor'—more than just equipment. It is a combination of people, procedures, systems and equipment. However, it is necessary to understand what a 'word processor' is, and what it can do, so that you can understand the effects using this equipment can have on people and office systems and office personnel.

Figure S2.1 shows a typical word processor. It has a **screen**, a **disk drive**, a **keyboard** and a **printer**.

There are many kinds of word processing system and they operate in various ways, but all of them have these four basic parts in one form or another. These four pieces of equipment are often termed a **work station**. With some types of system, where the disk drive and printer are shared, the screen and keyboard units at which the operator works make up the **work station**.

The screen, disk drive, keyboard and printer make up what is known as the **hardware** of a word processing system, which simply means that it is the equipment which can be seen and handled. The word processor operates by means of a **central processing unit (CPU)** and **memory**.

Figure S2.1 *Components of a typical word processor*

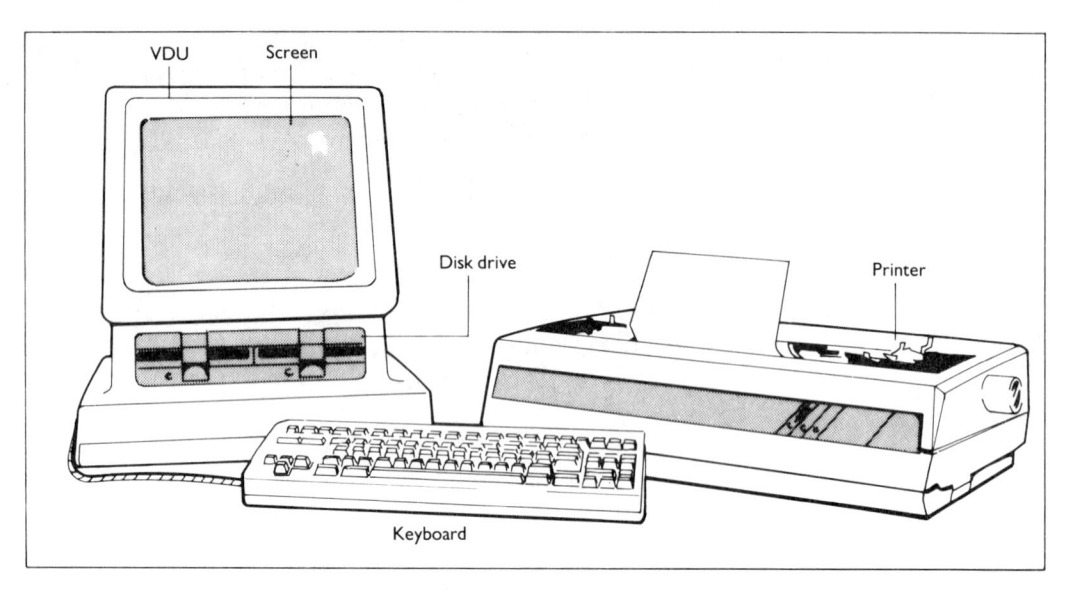

The memory

Software and memory

In addition to the hardware, a word processing system needs **software** in the form of a computer program which gives instructions to the word processor to enable it to carry out word processing functions. A word processor is in fact simply a computer that has been programmed to operate in a particular way. The word processing program is stored in the system's **memory**, so that operations can be carried out.

The central processing unit

The central processing unit, or **CPU**, is the computer that controls all the functions and operations of a word processing system. It comprises the processor and a certain amount of immediate storage—

usually called the memory—in which the programs reside while they are being run. The CPU enables the system to carry out the instructions that are given to it when the operator presses one or more keys.

Response time

Response time, or **access time**, is the length of time it takes for the word processing system to act upon an instruction given from the keyboard. A response time of two or three seconds may seem very quick, but if the operator has to wait three seconds or more for each instruction to be carried out, the operations will be slowed down to a point that causes frustration. A very quick response time is therefore desirable.

The visual display unit and screen

The visual display unit and screen

The word processing screen is fitted into a box-shaped unit which is often called a **visual display unit (VDU)** or a **video display terminal (VDT)**. A terminal is simply another name for the VDU or work station. Among other things, the screen shows the operator what has been typed, what margins have been set, and it may also display messages from the system to help and guide the operator.

There are two types of VDU terminal—dumb and intelligent. **Dumb terminals** allow the operator to send and receive information to a system while the central processing unit itself holds all the intelligence. **Intelligent terminals** incorporate 'intelligence' in the form of their own processors, which hold small programs. These can carry out certain functions and allow the operator to undertake basic processing work without involving the CPU.

Soft copy

Information displayed on the screen is often called **soft copy** by computer people. The term **hard copy** is used to describe the work once it has been printed out on paper. The soft copy appearing on the screen is generally referred to in word processing terms as **text**, and this text can be produced as hard copy on the printer.

Screen size

Most screens show a width of 80 characters across the screen and about 20 to 25 lines of text down the screen, which allows about half an A4 page of text to appear on the screen at any one time.

Full-page screens

Full-page screens are also available, showing a full A4 page of information, with the shorter edge of the A4 'page' at the top. Other systems may have a screen that allows the display of the full width of an A4 page with the longer edge at the top, so that wide documents may be seen on the screen as they will appear when printed out.

Scrolling

By pressing a key, the operator can move the text up and down on the screen to see the rest of the page. This is known as **scrolling**. On a good word processing system the scrolling is very smooth and the lines of type move slowly and evenly up or down the screen. Smooth scrolling is important for the operator, because it is less tiring to the eyes than a jerky movement.

Wide documents

Word processing systems which have an 80-character wide screen may permit the operator to type a wide document by allowing the text to be scrolled to the left or right for each line.

Character set

The size and shape of the characters on the screen are important, and these will vary from system to system. The characters should have **ascenders** and **descenders**—that is, the vertical strokes of characters such as 'h' and 'p' should extend above and below the line of type.

Colours

Screens are available with a range of colour combinations—green characters on a black background, green on brown, yellow on brown, white on black, black on white, etc.

Operator comfort

The design of the VDU is very important if the operator is to work in comfort. Some screens may be tilted or rotated from left to right so that they can be adjusted to suit the operator. A brightness control switch allows the operator to adjust the brightness of the display. Anti-glare screens may also be supplied on some word processing systems, or they may be purchased and fitted later if glare and reflections cause problems for the operator.

Fuller details about information which is displayed on the screen to help the operator during word processing operations are given on page 20–25.

The keyboard

The **keyboard** of a word processor may be built into the same unit as the screen, or it may be a separate component connected to the VDU by a cable, as shown in Fig. S2.1. A keyboard that is separate from the screen unit has advantages for the operator because it can be adjusted to the most comfortable position, and therefore reduce fatigue. Some manufacturers provide keyboards with adjustable legs, so that the keyboard can be tilted to the most convenient position for the operator.

Keying in

When the word processing operator is using the keyboard to type in text to the screen, this is generally called **keying in** rather than typing, because the actual 'typing' operation is not carried out until the printer is instructed to print out the documents.

Keyboard layout

The **layout** of the word processor keyboard is designed so that a trained typist can adapt to it with ease. It generally consists of the QWERTY alphabet and number keyboard found on the standard typewriter, with some additional keys—function keys, command keys, control keys or code keys— grouped around the QWERTY keys. In addition, some systems also have a **numeric keypad** at the right-hand side, arranged like the keys on a calculator, for use where a large number of figures have to be keyed in. On some systems, these number keys may also be used in conjunction with a code key as additional function keys, such as CENTRE, DELETE or INSERT, and they may be labelled with their function. An example of a typical word processor keyboard layout is shown in Fig. S2.2.

Other keyboard layouts are available, such as the MALTRON keyboard, on which the character keys are arranged in two groups of keys shaped to match the shape of the hands. However, the word processing operator will probably find that the QWERTY keyboard is the most commonly used keyboard.

Figure S2.2 *A typical word processor keyboard*

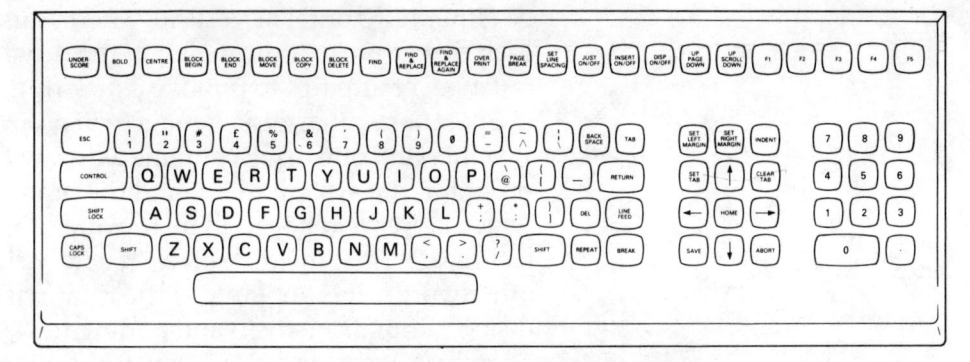

Function, command, control or code keys

These special keys tell the system what the operator wants the word processing system to do, in other words, what **function** or operation is to be carried out by the system. The operator is giving a **command**, or instruction, to the word processor. Some systems have special **dedicated keys**, which means the keys are dedicated to one particular function, such as DELETE, INSERT, CENTRE, UNDERLINE, and so on. The keys are often marked with the function name to help the operator work quickly and efficiently.

Instead of using dedicated keys, other systems may use a **code key**, in conjunction with alphabetic keys, to carry out functions such as delete, insert or centre. The operator presses the code key, followed by one or more of the alphabet or number keys from the QWERTY keyboard to carry out the special function. Systems such as this often use **mnemonics** (which simply means memory aids) to help the operator to remember which key to use for a particular function, such as D for delete, W for word, C for centre and so on. The names of these functions may be printed on the front of the alphabet keys to help the operator. Almost every character key may perform a separate function when it is pressed in association with the code key.

Many systems combine some dedicated function keys with the use of code keys plus alphabet keys in order to cover the wide range of functions that can be carried out on a sophisticated word processor. The systems that are easiest to use are those which involve the fewest keystrokes for any function.

EXECUTE key or ACTION key

When a command has been keyed into the system by pressing the appropriate keys, it will not be acted upon by the system until a special **ACTION key** is pressed. This ACTION key is often called the **EXECUTE key** (EXEC for short) because it executes, or carries out, the instruction just given. However, the name given to this key may vary from system to system. The **RETURN key** (which, on a typewriter would be called the carriage return key) is used as the EXECUTE key on some systems.

The disk drive

The **disk drive** is the mechanism that operates the storage disks which contain the word processing program and text which has been keyed in and stored.

The disk drive shown in Fig. S2.1 on page 6 is the type found on a typical standalone word processor. It consists of a unit with two apertures, or slots, into each of which a disk can be inserted. The disk drive may be housed beneath the screen, beside the screen or as a separate unit, and the apertures into which the disks are inserted may be either horizontal or vertical. There is usually a small red light on each disk drive to indicate when the drive is operating. The operator must never attempt to remove a disk from the drive while the drive is in operation, otherwise damage will occur.

Generally, one drive contains a disk with the word processing program (the **system disk**), and the other drive is used for the disk which stores text keyed in by the operator (the **working disk**). In technical terms, the disk drive 'reads' a disk and 'writes to' a disk. In other words, it is 'looking' at the information already stored on the disk (reading from disk) and adding new information when the operator keys in and stores text (writing to disk).

Word processors with two drives are known as dual disk drive systems. Some word processors have only one disk drive; these are known as single disk drive systems. Some word processors may have three disk drives.

The printer

There are many types of printer for use with a word processing system. They are generally divided into two types: **impact printers** and **non-impact printers**. Impact printers print by the striking action of a printhead through an inked ribbon. Non-impact printers do not strike through a ribbon, but print by some other means, such as spraying ink in the shape of the characters to be printed.

Some printers are able to print both forwards and backwards: these are known as **bi-directional printers**. They print one line from left to right, and every alternate line starting at the end of the line and ending at the left margin. Printing both forwards and backwards along the line in this way speeds up the printing operation. Some types of printer are able to produce line charts and graphs.

Impact printers

Impact printers include **daisy wheel, thimble, golfball** and **dot matrix printers**. They are able to operate at fairly high speeds. Daisy wheel and golfball printers produce good quality print and are often called **letter quality printers** because printed copies are of a standard that is acceptable for letters and other documents in a business office.

Because the print is formed by a striking action, it is possible to make carbon copies with an impact printer, or to use multi-part stationery.

Impact printers are fairly noisy, which can be a disadvantage in a busy office. However, an **acoustic hood** may be fitted over the printer to reduce the noise level. An acoustic hood is a specially-designed 'box', with a cover that can be lifted to allow the insertion of paper in the printer.

Daisy wheel and thimble printers

The majority of printers used on word processing systems are described as **daisy wheel printers**. Daisy wheel printers are impact printers. The printhead is a daisy-shaped disk made of metal or plastic that has the characters embossed on its 'petals'. As the disk spins a character is hammered against an inked ribbon to form the print on the paper. A printhead known as a **thimble** works in a similar way. Figure S2.3 shows a daisy wheel and a thimble printhead.

The daisy wheels or thimbles can be changed in a matter of seconds, so that the operator can change the **typestyle** and the **pitch** (size of print) to suit the type of document being printed. Examples of different typestyles and pitch are shown in Fig. S2.4.

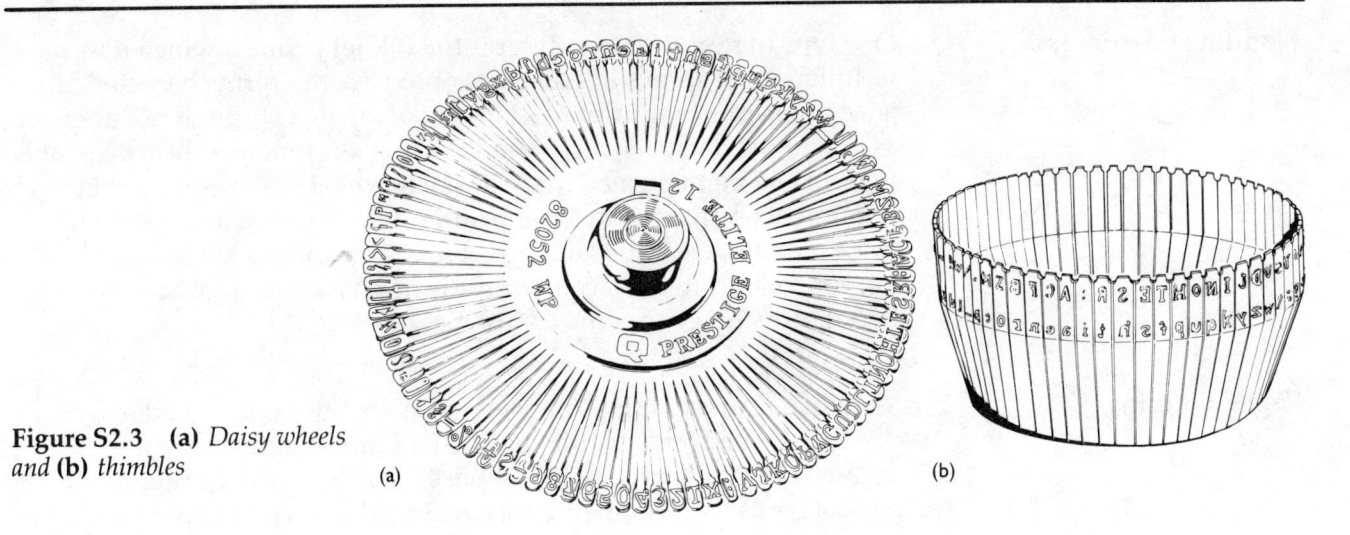

Figure S2.3 (a) Daisy wheels and (b) thimbles

Figure S2.4 Typestyles and pitches (Courtesy INMAC UK Ltd.)

Golfball printers	A small number of word processing systems use the **golfball printhead** which is used on some electric typewriters. The golfball impact printer is relatively slow compared with the daisy wheel printer, but it has the same advantages of a rapid change of printhead to allow different typestyles and pitch sizes to be used.
Dot matrix printers	The **dot matrix printer** is an impact printer of a type that is often supplied with a microcomputer for computer purposes, but which may also be used with a word processing system. Patterns of tiny dots are printed on the page to form the characters, and the pitch and typestyle may be changed very simply, without any need to change printheads. The quality of print produced varies, and on some matrix printers it is not considered as letter quality, suitable for business correspondence. However, some matrix printers can produce a very acceptable standard of print.

Some dot matrix printers can operate at speeds higher than the daisy wheel printers. Because of this high-speed capability, some companies with a very heavy usage of word processing have both daisy wheel and dot matrix printers fitted to their word processing systems. The dot matrix printer may be used to produce draft copies at high speed, leaving the daisy wheel printers free to produce final copies of a higher quality.

Non-impact printers

One type of **non-impact printer** is the **ink jet printer**, which uses a technique that sprays ink droplets onto paper to form characters. Ink jet printers produce print of a fairly good quality, though not as good as that of the daisy wheel printer. The ink jet printer is, however, able to print at a higher speed than the daisy wheel systems. Another non-impact printer is the **laser printer**, which uses a laser beam to print the characters. It is not possible to take carbon copies with non-impact printers, because there is no striking action, and this may be a disadvantage to some companies.

Paper handling

Many word processing printers require the operator to feed in a sheet of paper whenever a document is to be printed out. Where a high volume of work is produced it is possible to have the printer fitted with a **sheet feeder** or a **hopper**, which will hold a stack of paper and automatically feed one sheet at a time into the printer. Alternatively, a special **tractor feed** may be used which will enable the operator to use **continuous stationery**. A diagram of a sheet feeder and a tractor feed printer are shown in Fig. S2.5 (a) and (b).

Figure S2.5 (a) *A sheet feeder/hopper feed and* (b) *a tractor feed printer*

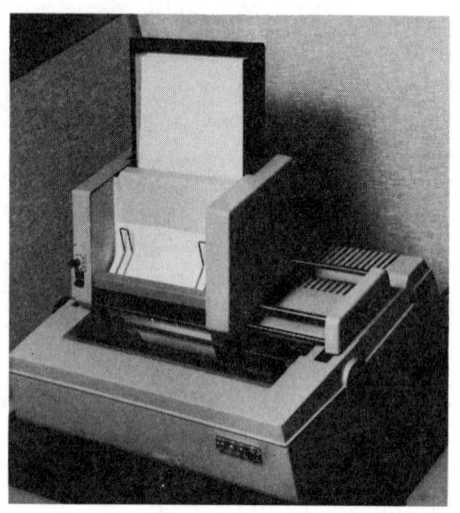

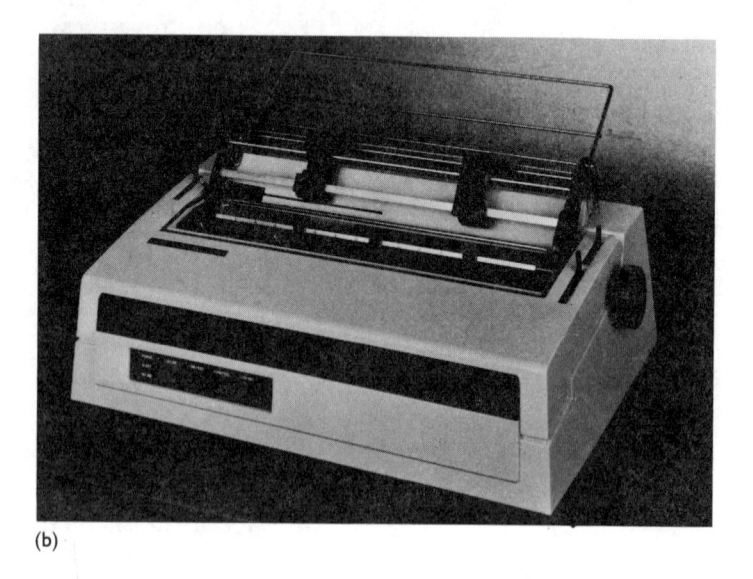

Storage media

There are four main types of magnetic storage media currently in use—floppy disks or diskettes, hard disks, magnetic cards and magnetic tape cassettes. Information is stored **randomly** on floppy disks and hard disks and is retrieved by **random access**, which means that the information can be retrieved very rapidly. Cassette tape and cards have the disadvantage that information is stored **serially** in the order it is input to the system. With these serial forms of storage media, information can only be read by going through all the stored information in the order of input until the required point is reached. This is called **serial access**, and the disadvantage is that serial access of information is slow.

Floppy disks or diskettes

The type of disk used on many standalone word processors is often called a **floppy disk or diskette** (see Fig. S2.6) because it is made from a flexible material. A floppy disk is a flat, circular piece of material with a

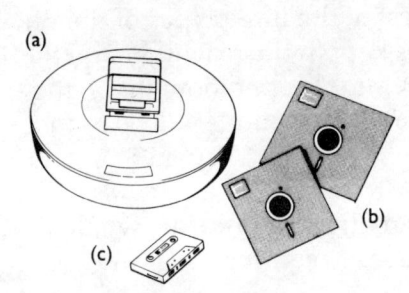

Figure S2.6 (a) *Hard disks,* (b) *floppy disks and* (c) *cassettes*

magnetisable surface on which information can be stored. The disk itself is permanently sealed in a special envelope-type cover that protects the disk and makes it easier for the operator to handle it without causing damage.

Floppy disks come in various sizes—8 inch, $5\frac{1}{4}$ inch and even smaller disks called **minidisks**. These disks may be capable of storing information on one side or on both sides. Disks may also be **double-density** or **single-density**, the double-density disks being able to store more information on the same size of disk than the single-density disk.

The disks are inserted into the appropriate drives at the start of a word processing session, and removed when the system is closed down at the end of the working day. Disks should be very carefully handled and stored. Where the system uses floppy disks, the operator is likely to be in control of the disks, as far as looking after the disks, inserting them into the machine and removing them is concerned.

Hard disks

Some word processing systems operate with **hard disks**, which are much larger than floppy disks and capable of storing a very much larger quantity of information than the floppy disks (see Fig. S2.6). Thousands of pages of text can be stored on one hard disk.

Where a system uses hard disks, the control of the disks is likely to be in the care of a systems manager, and the operator will be unlikely to see or handle them.

Cassette tape and card

Magnetic tape cassettes, similar to those used on an ordinary tape recorder but of a higher quality, may be used in connection with word processors. **Magnetic cards** are small playing-card sized cards. Both tape and card storage media have the disadvantages of storing only small quantities of information, and slow retrieval of information, and their use is limited.

Consumable items

A number of items should be kept in stock for use with word processing equipment. These items, which are retained until they are used or broken, are generally known as **consumable** items of stock.

Printheads

The **printhead** is the daisy wheel, thimble or golfball unit that carries the print characters. Instructions for changing the printhead will be found in the manufacturer's manual, supplied with the word processor.

The operator will usually have a supply of printheads of various typestyles and type sizes. The sizes of type commonly used are 10, 12 and 15 pitch (being 10, 12 and 15 characters to the inch) and proportional spacing. Figure S2.4 on page 11 illustrates some of the typestyles and pitches available.

Ribbons

Ribbons are available in various types, depending on the quality required. Single-strike carbon film is a high-quality ribbon, which is called a **single-pass ribbon** because it goes through the printer only once, each character being printed on a fresh piece of film as it advances. **Multi-strike ribbon** is also a single-pass ribbon, but it lasts four times as long as the single-strike ribbon because it advances a quarter of a character at a time, so there is some overlap between used and unused ribbon for each letter. **Continuous loop** is an inked fabric

	ribbon, usually nylon, and is the cheapest of the three types of ribbon. It can be used over and over again and is kept in the machine until the ink dries up. Changing a ribbon is a very simple operation, involving the changing of a cartridge or cassette, and instructions will be found in the operating manual.
Disks	A supply of unused floppy disks (or magnetic tape or cards, where these are used) will need to be kept for use as required.
Storage units	A storage box or file will be required in which to store disks currently in use.
Anti-static cleaner	An anti-static cleaning fluid is used to wipe over the screen and the casing of the equipment, both to clean it and to reduce static electricity which attracts dust to the terminal.
Stationery	A supply of plain and headed stationery of varying sizes and qualities should be maintained in storage units in the word processing room.

Review questions

1. Identify the four main components of a word processor.
2. What do the following initials stand for: CPU, VDU, VDT?
3. What features of a VDU can contribute to the comfort of a word processing operator?

Activity

Write a review of your system, identifying the type of system and commenting on screen size, keyboard layout and other features discussed in Section 2.

SECTION 3 SOME TYPES OF WORD PROCESSING SYSTEM

Word processing may be undertaken on many different types of system. The advance of technology is so rapid that the distinctions that once existed between various types of equipment are now less obvious. Machines that were originally designed to undertake computing/data processing tasks can also act as word processors. Equipment that was originally designed solely and specifically to do word processing may now also be able to undertake computing/data processing functions.

Electronic typewriters

Some sophisticated types of electronic typewriter have the capability to store information in memory. Some may also be provided with external storage in the form of a disk drive and floppy disks. A single line display 'screen' may be provided, called a **thin window display**, on which several words of a line of type may be displayed at any one time (Fig. S3.1)

Figure S3.1 *Thin window display*

```
an example of a 'thin window display' ...
```

Electronic typewriters of this type are able to carry out a number of text editing functions and simple word processing operations, but they cannot be considered as true word processors. If there is a distinction to be made between sophisticated electronic typewriters and basic word processing systems, it is that a true word processing system has a VDU screen that will display 20 or more lines of text at a time. Figure S3.2 shows an electronic text editing typewriter with external memory.

Figure S3.2 *Electronic text editing typewriter with external memory and single line display*

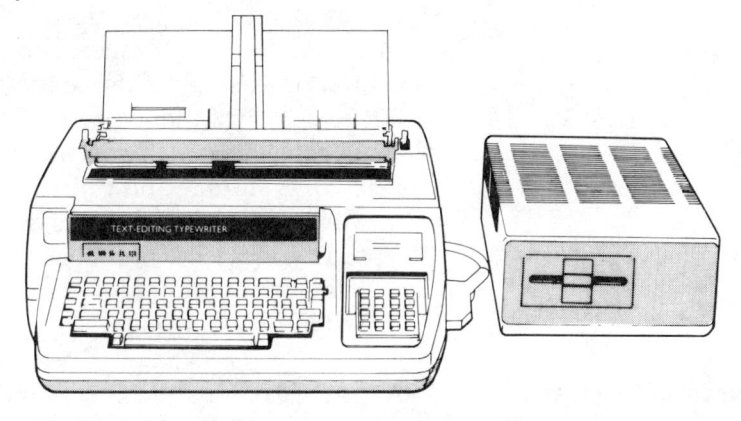

Dedicated and standalone word processors

The term **dedicated word processor** refers to equipment that has been designed specifically to carry out word processing functions. In other words, the machine is dedicated to the task of word processing. The keyboard is designed with word processing functions in mind, with special dedicated keys to carry out various commands. Operating such a system is quicker and easier than using a system that does not have these dedicated function keys.

The majority of the first dedicated word processors were **standalone** systems. This simply meant that they were self-contained and did not need to be connected to any other equipment for operating purposes.

A standalone machine has all the elements needed to operate—a screen, keyboard, central processing unit, disk drive and printer. Figure S2.1 page 6 shows a typical dedicated standalone word processor. Many of the newer types of dedicated word processing system are able to operate with programs that enable them to function as data processing computers, as well as word processors.

Although many of the more recently produced word processors are standalone systems, they are generally designed so that they can communicate with other equipment such as a central computer system or other word processors, or be linked together to share resources such as CPUs and printers.

Shared resource and shared logic systems

Shared resource word processors differ from standalone equipment because two or more VDUs share resources such as storage and printers. In shared resource systems the VDU terminals must be intelligent terminals with their own microprocessors. Some shared resource systems can operate 30 or more work stations and a number of printers from one CPU. Figure S3.3 shows an example of a shared resource system.

Figure S3.3 *A shared resource system*

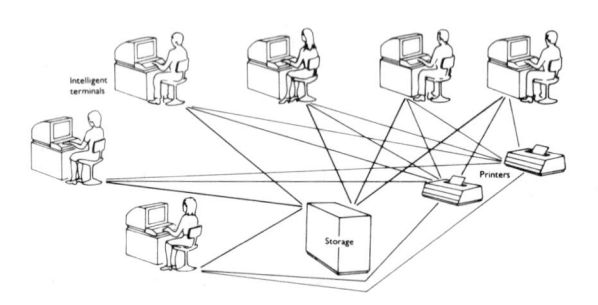

Various terms have been used to describe systems to which the overall name **shared resource systems** can be applied. **Shared logic** refers to those systems in which several work stations are connected individually to the central logic unit, the CPU. The term **shared facility** generally refers to systems in which several work stations share printers and disk storage, where the work stations may have their own central processing units, or they may simply consist of VDUs and keyboards. Another term used is **distributed cluster system**, which again refers to systems in which a number of work stations share a CPU, disk storage and printers.

Word processing systems in which several work stations operate from a central logic unit generally store information on a **hard disk**, which enables operators to share access to a very large quantity of stored information.

Microcomputer-based systems

A great deal of word processing is carried out in business using **microcomputers** which have been designed to carry out data processing functions. The microcomputer carries out those data processing functions by means of computer programs. By using a specially-written word processing computer program, the microcomputer can be used to carry out word processing functions in the same way as a word processor. Figure S3.4 on page 17 shows a microcomputer.

One of the disadvantages of using a microcomputer for word processing may be that, because the keyboard is designed for data processing, it does not have special function keys dedicated to such operations as centring, underlining or deleting. A sequence of several alphabet character keys may be needed to carry out a function such as centring, which might be a matter of pressing only one or two keys on a dedicated word processor. However, it is possible to purchase a specially-designed dedicated word processing keyboard for some microcomputers, if word processing is the main function for which the computer is to be used.

Microcomputers may be linked, or networked, together to share resources such as the CPU and printers, and a hard disk may be used at a central station instead of floppy disks at the individual work stations.

Figure S3.4 *A microcomputer*

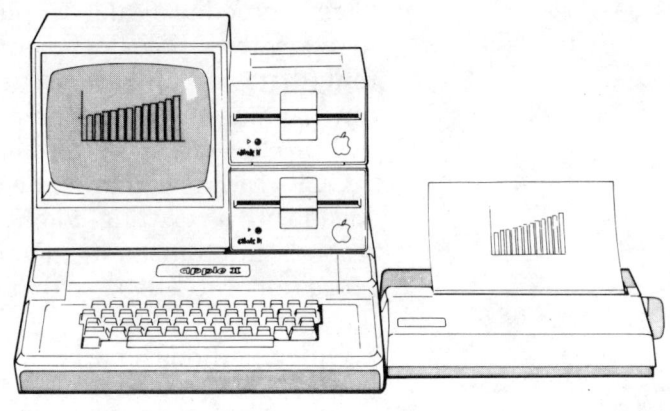

Minicomputer or mainframe computer-based systems

A **mainframe** computer is a large computer that is used for large-scale computing operations such as preparation of wages, stock control, data processing, etc. A **minicomputer** is also a computer that is used for large-scale computing operations. A minicomputer is smaller and less powerful than a mainframe computer, but it should not be confused with a microcomputer which is small enough to sit on a desk top.

A minicomputer or mainframe computer may, in addition to its data processing operations, be **accessed** or used for word processing, if a word processing program is available. In this case, the word processing work station consists of a VDU with a keyboard, together with a printer which may be shared with two or three other work stations. The work stations may be in a separate room quite distant from the main computer and linked to it only by cables.

The mainframe and minicomputer differ from the dedicated word processing equipment and microcomputers in their capacity to handle a very large amount of different types of work simultaneously. A word processor, or a microcomputer with the appropriate technical features, may be used for either word processing or data processing, but not for both at once. However, a large computer may have a very large number of terminals in use at the same time, some of them being operated for data processing and some for word processing. This is sometimes known as a **time-sharing** system of word processing.

Networking

Local area networking (LAN) is a method of linking office systems together by means of a special cable to increase productivity, and it is a step towards the integrated electronic office. The developments of technology have led to the introduction of a great variety of equipment—electronic typewriters, word processors, facsimile (FAX) equipment, photocopiers, telex machines, computers and so on. These machines were all designed to carry out specific tasks, but it has become increasingly obvious that offices would operate more efficiently if the machines could all be connected and communicate with each other.

Networking enables the different pieces of office equipment to communicate with each other and to make use of the facilities of other equipment. Information may be keyed in on one machine, stored on another, printed out on a third piece of equipment or sent to various other network users.

Alternative methods of input

The initials **OCR** stand for **optical character recognition**. The OCR technique is a means of transferring typed information straight from the page and into a word processing system. In this way, an existing page of typed text can be input to the word processor without the need to re-key the whole document. The typed material must be typed in a **font** (that is the character set or typestyle) which the OCR equipment can 'read' or recognise, and a good black print is also required, such as that produced by a carbon film ribbon.

OCR-reading equipment works by scanning the typed page at high speed with a very bright light. The reader can scan an A4 page in a few seconds and transfer it either directly to the screen of the word processor or to a disk, so that it can be transferred to the screen when the operator is ready.

Other methods have been developed to ensure that the operator's time is spent on word processing functions and not on initial keying in of text. Small units are available which may be linked to a typewriter to enable it to write or input directly onto floppy disks. This means that original keying in may be done by a typist, and the disks can then be passed to the word processing operator and used on the word processing system in the normal way.

Another manufacturer has developed a unit that comprises a standard keyboard with some word processing function keys, a single line thin window display and a recorder that stores several pages of text on a microcassette tape. Documents can be prepared on this unit and the information on the recorded tape transferred onto the VDU screen of the word processor so that the operator can read and amend it.

An alternative approach is intended for use by the executive rather than the typist or operator. It is a small hand-held unit with only six keys which are used in combination to input characters and various basic text editing commands, such as centring. The user can key in text, which is stored in the memory or on a magnetic cassette tape and which can then be transferred directly to a word processor or printed out on an electronic typewriter or printer.

Voice recognition

The electronic office of the future may not need operators keying in text to a typewriter or word processor. The executive or the secretary will simply speak into a microphone and the words as they are spoken will appear directly on the screen. Corrections or amendments may be made to the document on the screen, before it is transmitted electronically to its destination. Some advances have been made towards this 'ideal' office, but there is a long way to go before voice-activated equipment is perfected. Some computers and voice-activated typewriters can already recognise human speech and respond to a range of instructions, and some equipment is able to 'talk back' to the operator, with synthesised speech.

Voice input

A technique called **voice input** should not be confused with voice recognition. Voice input generally refers to a method of incorporating dictated words with stored text, so that it can be recalled by the operator when the relevant text appears on the screen. A signal will tell the operator that there is a voice message related to a particular item on the screen, and the message may ask the operator to check or change certain figures. The voice input facility may be used by an executive to respond to a memo sent by electronic mail. The executive can read a memo displayed on the screen, add a voice input message to say 'Thanks, I've noted the figures' and electronically 'mail' the memo back to the original author.

Selection of a system

The choice of the most suitable word processing system for a company depends on many factors—the price, the degree of sophistication required, the ease with which the system may be expanded, the storage capacity, the ease of use, the reliability of the manufacturer's maintenance and service back-up, the quality of training provided and many other features. Selection of a system that will meet all the company's requirements within the amount of money it is able to spend is not a simple matter. A detailed study of the company's needs in terms of the type of work undertaken must be made, together with a thorough investigation of the systems available on the market.

Review questions

1. Outline the difference between a dedicated standalone word processing system and a shared resource system.
2. List some of the factors that may influence a company in the choice of a word processing system.
3. Name three different types of word processing system available.

Activity

Draw a diagram of an office layout for a word processing centre in a large organisation with a shared resource system, including a CPU and 20 work stations sharing five printers.

SECTION 4 USING A WORD PROCESSING SYSTEM

When a word processor is used, the information is keyed in and the characters appear on the screen as they are keyed, without being printed. Corrections or changes can be made as words are keyed in or at any later stage. The text can be printed immediately or it may be stored on a disk for later use. Information that has been stored can be instantly retrieved and called back to the screen for review, change or printing, without re-keying the whole document. Printing takes place independently, leaving the operator free to continue editing another document or to create a new document.

Manufacturers of word processing equipment emphasise the simplicity of operation of the systems they design and sell, and try to ensure that the system is designed to help the operator. Much of this help comes to the operator in the form of **operator aids** or **operator prompts** on the VDU screen. These operator aids take the form of instructions and messages which are either on the screen all the time the system is operating or which appear when the operator needs some guidance. In addition, the system may give audio signals in the form of **bleeps** to draw the operator's attention to a screen message.

The screen messages appear in special 'blocks' or 'lines' at the top or bottom of the screen. There is no standard method of naming these blocks or lines, but the terms **operator instruction line, prompt line** and **status line** are commonly used. In addition, a number of operator aids are displayed on the screen to help the operator.

Operator aids on the screen

The cursor

The **cursor** is a small square or line that appears on the screen to show the point at which keying in of text would take place if the operator started to type. On some word processing systems the cursor 'blinks' or 'flashes' on and off so that the operator can find it rapidly.

The cursor may be moved rapidly about the screen—up, down, forwards, backwards—by means of cursor movement keys, or cursor control keys on the keyboard.

Status line

On many word processing systems a line at the top of the screen constantly displays **status information** which tells (or reminds) the operator of the current 'state' of the work being done. On some systems, the status line may appear at the bottom of the screen.

The details shown on the status line will vary from system to system. However, a typical example given in Fig. S4.1 shows the mode or function being carried out (in this case creating or drafting a document), the name of the document being worked on, the page number, the line number of the line at which the cursor is currently resting and the position of the cursor along the line.

Figure S4.1 *A typical status line*

```
CREATE  sales  letter        Page 1 Line 5        Cursor 72
```

WORD PROCESSING—SYSTEMS, APPLICATIONS AND ASSIGNMENTS

The information on the status line will change as the mode or function changes and as the document is being keyed in. There may be two or more status lines on some types of word processor, containing information on page size, margin settings, tab settings, etc. On different systems, these status lines may be called a **ruler line**, a **tab rack**, a **control line** or a **format line** and they may be displayed on the screen all the time, or called up by the operator when he/she wants to look at them.

Ruler line

Most systems allow left- and right-hand margins and tabs to be set and these may be shown on a **ruler line**. The ruler line usually shows a scale, similar to the scale on a typewriter, marked out in tens. The left margin is usually indicated by L, the right by R and tab stops by T (see Fig. S4.2). Additional characters may be used to indicate such things as justified margins or decimal tab stops. Alternative names for the ruler may be the **tab rack**, or the **control line**.

Figure S4.2 *A typical ruler line*

```
25    30    35    40    45    50    55    60    65    70    75
..............................................................
L     T                             T                        R
```

More then one ruler line may be set in one page of a document if it is desired to change the margin settings and tabs at various points in the document.

The ruler may be permanently displayed on the screen, and on such systems a **dummy cursor** may move along the ruler line to show the current position of the cursor.

Format line

Information concerning the type size (pitch) to be used, the line spacing, the paper size, etc., must be given to the system before the text can be printed out. This information makes up what is known as the **format** or **layout** of a document. The necessary details may be given to the system either by means of the format line, or, on some systems by means of a **print menu**. More than one format line may be inserted or set throughout a page of text, in order to change the instructions to the system concerning these items. Figure S4.3 shows typical information which may be displayed on a format line.

Figure S4.3 *A typical format line*

```
Page length 11.75 in    Page width 8.25 in    Pitch 12
```

Prompt lines

On fairly sophisticated systems, a series of **prompts** consisting of either questions or instructions will appear in the status line or in a special **prompt line** to help guide the operator. The prompts may, for example, lead the operator through an involved **command sequence** of keystrokes. They may also give the operator instructions if an incorrect key has accidentally been pressed, and in such a case the prompts may be called **error messages**.

Menus

Many systems display a **menu** of options or choices of action from which the operator may select the desired option by pressing a command key. Menus should provide the maximum help and guidance without slowing down the operator's rate of work. It is possible on some systems for the menus to be bypassed once the operator has become proficient in using the system, the function required being selected without bringing the menu onto the screen display.

Menu-type word processing systems generally have a **main menu**. They may also have a **print menu** and other **sub-menus** to help guide the operator through the system's operations as easily as possible. Figure S4.4 shows a typical main menu.

Figure S4.4 *A typical main menu*

```
                      MAIN MENU

         C   Create a document    P  Print a document
         CO  Copy a document      R  Re-name a document
         D   Delete a document    S  Spelling check
         E   Edit a document      X  Exit from system
         I   Index of documents
```

Index

Most word processing systems automatically prepare and maintain an **index** of all documents that have been stored on a disk. When a document is to be created on the screen, it is always given a name by the operator and the system automatically adds this name to the index list. The operator can then later refer to the index to find and recall any document required. Some systems will automatically rearrange the index in alphabetical order whenever a new document is added and record the date on which the document was created or amended. Some systems allow additional information to be included on the index list, such as the name of the author of a document. When a document is deleted from the file storage, the document name will also be removed from the index list. An example of one type of index of documents is given in Fig. S4.5.

Figure S4.5 *An index of documents*

```
                            INDEX

       DOC   TITLE                    AUTHOR       DATE
       NO                                          CREATED

       27    annual sales figures     J Browne     23/11/198-
       28    development plan report  K Mather     12/09/198-
       29    standard letter          E Sanders    03/12/198-
       30    telephone list           H Benson     15/01/198-
       31    vehicle record           A Ginsberg   07/08/198-
```

Blinking and highlighting

Blinking is the term used when characters are made to flash on the screen, in order to draw the operator's attention to a particular part of the screen. **Reverse video**, or **inverse video**, is another method of drawing attention to a particular part of the screen to highlight certain features. The parts of the screen highlighted with reverse video have dark characters on a light background, instead of the usual light characters on a dark background. The status line is usually highlighted with reverse video.

End of text marker

The screen may display a signal or marker to identify the end of the text, so that the operator knows where the last characters of the document appear. Instead of a signal, the system may show the words END OF TEXT.

Service codes and trace codes

Service codes or **trace codes** are special marker signals displayed on the screen to remind the operator of various commands that have been carried out. A small triangle ◀ may, for example, indicate the end of a paragraph which has been made by pressing the RETURN key; a 'box' around the first character of a heading may indicate that the heading was centred by means of a special centring command; and a dot may indicate each blank character space on the screen. Some screens display these service codes at all times. Other systems show just a few of the service codes, such as 'end of paragraph' and 'end of text' markers, at all times, all the other service codes being invisible until the operator wishes to call them up by pressing a special command key. This causes the system to display the text on the screen together with the service codes.

The ability to view the service or trace codes is very useful when the operator is trying to trace operating problems that may have arisen in working on a document, or in planning the layout of a complicated piece of work.

Help files

Some systems are able to give help to the operator in the form of **help files**. If the operator is not able to remember the correct procedure to carry out a particular function, such as centring a heading, for example, the HELP key can be pressed to ask the system for guidance. The system will display on the screen an operator prompt giving a reminder of the sequence of keystrokes necessary to carry out the function. In effect, the system carries an abbreviated form of the operating manual, which the operator can refer to on the screen rather than taking time to look up the procedure in the printed manual.

Keying in text

When the operator types material in to the word processor this is known as **keying in** rather than typing. The material that is keyed in is known as **text**, both when it appears on the screen and when it has been printed out. The operator keys in characters, and line after line of text appears on the screen without being printed. The text is recorded and stored on disk, and the operator will print out what has been keyed in only when the work has been satisfactorily completed.

Wraparound or word wrap

As the operator types a line of text, the system automatically makes the decision that the end of a line has been reached. If a word is too long to fit on the line, it is automatically carried down to the next line. This means that the operator does not need to press the RETURN key at the end of each line. In fact, it is important that the operator does *not* press the RETURN key at the end of a line unless a new paragraph is required. This word wrap facility speeds up the keying in process.

Hard return

Using the RETURN key inserts a line ending known as a **hard return**. The RETURN key is pressed at the end of a heading, at the end of a paragraph, or at the end of a sentence in existing text if a new paragraph is required. The RETURN key is also pressed at the end of each line of a tabulated statement and where an extra line space is required. To help the operator, a service code symbol may be displayed on the screen at the point where the return was operated to show that a hard return has been made.

Blank space and hard space

One of the most important things a new operator has to learn is the difference between the function of the space bar and the functions of the cursor control keys. When the space bar is operated, a **hard space** is inserted into the text, so if the operator wants to insert a space—between words, for example—the space bar should be pressed. As far as the word processing system is concerned, the hard space is a 'character' that must be stored on the disk like any alphabet character.

When the operator wishes to move the cursor around the screen, the cursor control keys should be pressed and the cursor will move over characters and spaces *without* keying in blank hard spaces. This is, in fact, straightforward, but the new operator will often press the space bar in an effort to move the cursor forward and will become confused when extra blank spacing appears. A little practice is necessary to remember when to use the cursor control keys and when to use the space bar.

Scrolling

When the operator has keyed in more text than can be displayed on the screen at any one time, the text moves up the screen and disappears from view. However, it is still held by the word processor ready for viewing and by pressing a cursor control key the operator can cause the text to move back down the screen again so that it can be seen and read—and if necessary altered. The operator can **scroll** the text up and down, and on some systems from side to side if a wide document is being prepared.

Page markers

A word processing system is programmed so that it allocates an equal number of lines of text to each page of a document when it is printed out. When text is being keyed in, a word processor will operate either on a page basis or a document basis. On a word processor that operates on a page basis, the system will automatically decide when enough text, together with top and bottom margins, has been keyed in to occupy a page. Any following text will automatically begin on a new page in the system.

On systems that work on a document basis, the operator keys in the whole document, which may consist of enough text to occupy one, two or several pages of text, without worrying about where the end of a page will come. When the keying in of the document has been completed, the operator will use the automatic **paging function** on the word processing system to allocate text to pages. The system will go through the document and divide it into page lengths. The division of pages is shown on the screen, and this may be in the form of a broken line, or of a line with the words **page marker** included.

The operator can view the document after it has been **paged**, and decide whether the end of a page comes at an appropriate point. If the text has been divided at an inappropriate point, such as halfway through a table of figures, the operator can change the position of the 'end of page' marker. Pagination of longer documents can require some skill and expertise in using the word processing system and its pagination functions.

Housekeeping

The term **housekeeping** generally refers to various functions connected with the storage of text on the disks: naming documents, location of documents on the disks, deletion of unwanted documents, amount of space available and security copying. At its simplest level, it means that the operator should maintain the information stored on the disks in such a way that it is always quick and easy to find any document required, in much the same way that a secretary keeps a filing cabinet logically ordered and up-to-date.

When a document is being created, the operator must give it a name, which should be explanatory enough to identify the document even if the operator is looking for it some weeks or months later. It may be useful if the name or initials of the author are included in the name.

Disks should be labelled clearly to indicate what is stored on them and separate disks may be used for different types of work—one for reports, one for letters, etc. The operator may use a colour code to identify disks—green labels, for example, identifying disks that contain reports and blue labels for standard letters, etc.

An important housekeeping function is the deletion or removal of unwanted documents from the disk in accordance with instructions given. Documents that are no longer required should be deleted so that it is quicker to identify on the index a document that is wanted and so that the space may be re-used for new documents.

The operator should also check, before starting work on a disk, how much space is left on the disk to see whether it is worth starting a new job on that particular disk or if a new one should be used. This can usually be discovered by 'asking' the system how much space is left. The answer is usually in terms of the number of pages of space left on the disk. Some systems tell the operator when the disk is nearly full. It is usually suggested that about 25 pages should be left unused on a disk to allow for possible future amendments and additions to existing text.

On many systems the operator is able to print out a copy of the index of documents stored on a disk, and it is useful for future reference to keep a printed copy of the up-to-date index contents with each disk.

In many offices it is general practice for the operator to copy the information stored on a disk onto a **duplicate disk** in case the original should be lost or damaged.

Review questions

1. Briefly describe the word wrap or wraparound facility.
2. List four instances in which it is necessary for the operator to press the RETURN key instead of using the word wrap facility.
3. What housekeeping functions should be carried out by the operator?

Activity

Write a review of your word processing system, describing the features it provides on the screen in the form of operator aids, as outlined in Section 4.

SECTION 5 WHAT CAN A WORD PROCESSOR DO?

Word processors can carry out a very wide range of operations, some systems being able to carry out more extensive and more complicated procedures than others. The number of functions that can be undertaken on any particular word processor will depend on the equipment and the word processing program that has been written for that equipment.

Most word processors carry out a fairly standard range of basic text editing functions and a large number of such functions are described in detail in the practical assignment section of this book. An operator who has a sound understanding of, and ability to use, the basic operations of a word processing system can progress with confidence to learning the more advanced features and can adapt easily to any other system.

The things a word processor can do may be divided into five main areas:

– basic text editing;
– advanced word processing functions;
– records processing;
– mathematical functions;
– communications operations.

A number of the major operations that can be carried out in these five main areas are outlined below.

Basic text editing functions

Capitals Some word processors are able to change words, sentences or paragraphs that have been typed in lower case into capitals at the touch of only two or three special keys.

Centring A line of text or a whole block of text may be automatically centred between the left and right margins.

Corrections The operator can correct any typing errors by 'backspacing' over them, or by using the DELETE key. The characters are removed from the screen and the correct characters may then be keyed in. Errors may be corrected immediately as they are made, or at a later stage if the error is noticed sometime later.

Cut and paste A section of text may be removed from the screen, saved temporarily in a special memory section and then recalled from the memory to be 'pasted' back on the screen in a different position. This enables the operator to make large changes to the text without the need for re-typing.

Deleting If the operator wishes to remove some of the text that appears on the screen, it can be deleted, which means that it disappears from the screen and from the memory. A single character, word, sentence, paragraph or even a whole page may be deleted at the touch of two or three keys.

Emboldening	Text that is emboldened, or in bold print, is printed out darker and thicker than the rest of the text.
Format	The format function enables the operator to set up the **format** of the page of text to be produced. The format includes such items as the page length, page width, pitch (size of type) to be used, margins, line spacing, tabulation and printing requirements.
Hyphenating	When a long word is keyed in towards the end of a line, the word may be too long to fit on the line and it will automatically be wrapped to the next line. This might leave a long gap at the end of the line, and the operator may wish to hyphenate the word. Some systems automatically insert hyphens where they are required. Other systems allow the operator to insert what are termed **soft hyphens** or **optional hyphens**, which will disappear if the format is later altered so that the whole word can appear on one line.
Indent	If the operator wishes to inset text from the left margin, or from both the left and right margins, this may be done, on some word processors, with the indent function rather than by changing the right and left margin positions on the ruler line.
Justification	This function allows text to be printed out with an even right-hand margin, giving the appearance of printed matter.
Movement around the text	The operator is able to move rapidly to any point on the text shown on the screen with the aid of **cursor movement keys**—the cursor being a small signal on the screen that indicates the typing position. The system may be commanded to 'go to' the top or bottom of the document, or to any specific page of the document being worked on. The 'previous page' and 'next page' or 'previous screen' and 'next screen' command allows the operator to view the page or screenful of text immediately before and after the one currently being worked on. These functions enable the operator to move quickly through a document to make any necessary revisions or amendments.
Moving text	Text may be moved from one part of a document to another part of the same document. The operator can also take text from one document and move it to another document.
Pagination	On a system that operates on a 'document' basis, the text is keyed in without any decisions being made about where each page should end. Once the document has been keyed in, the word processing system is able to divide the text up into page lengths. The operator may over-ride the automatic pagination decisions made by the system to ensure, for example, that a table is not divided between two pages. Some systems work on a 'page' basis, in which text is keyed in until a page is full. However, if a long document is keyed in and later revised to include extra text throughout the document, the operator will need to use the re-pagination function of the word processing system to adjust the text into page lengths again.
Tabulation	Tabulated statements may be keyed in very simply with the aid of automatic alignment tabular stops, which align columns of numbers on a decimal point position. Special tab stops may also be used to key

in columns of words or figures so that they are aligned to the left, to the right or with each line centred.

Underlining — A character, word or any amount of text may be printed out with underlining.

Wraparound or word wrap — When keying in text, the operator does not need to operate a RETURN key at the end of a line of type, as with ordinary typewriting. The operator types continuously and the system decides where the end of a line should come, wrapping the next word onto the following line. This is known as the **word wrap** or **wraparound** facility.

Advanced word processing functions

The majority of word processing systems include all, or most of, the basic text editing functions listed above, but the more advanced word processing functions may not be available on all equipment. A number of advanced word processing functions are described below. Some word processing systems may include only a few of these facilities, while more sophisticated systems may include all of them and may possibly incorporate additional features.

Diagrams — Simple graphics, charts and diagrams such as organisation charts may be prepared on some word processors that have the facility to draw vertical, horizontal and, in some cases, diagonal lines on the screen. This function requires a printer that is able to print out the charts and diagrams that have been prepared on the screen.

Footnotes — This function allows the operator to include footnotes in a document with a reference symbol in the text and the footnote placed at the bottom of the page containing the reference. The system ensures that the footnote is printed on the page containing the reference.

Forms — Some word processors allow the operator to set up and, if required, print out forms. These forms may later be recalled to the screen to be completed with appropriate information and printed out.

Headers and footers — The **header** function allows the operator to key in information that is to be included at the top of every page, within the normal top margin, when it is printed. This header may include the title of a report, the date and the page number—or any other information required.

The **footer** function allows the operator to enter information that is to be included at the bottom of each page, within the normal bottom margin, when the document is printed, in exactly the same way as the header command.

Page numbering — When a long document has been keyed in, the pages may be automatically numbered by the system, either at the top or at the foot of the page. This page numbering function is very useful if new paragraphs are added to the document or others deleted, because the system will automatically re-number the pages.

Paragraph numbering — Paragraphs may, if desired, be automatically numbered by the word processor in various systems of numbering—decimal numbering or Roman or arabic numerals. If extra paragraphs are inserted (or deleted) during revision of a document, the system will automatically renumber all the paragraphs without further instruction from the operator.

Phrase storage	The **phrase storage facility** allows the operator to store a large number of frequently used phrases on disk in a special file. This might be the name of the company or the complimentary close of a letter. By keying in a command plus a number or an alphabetic character code, the operator can recall the phrase to the screen to be inserted in the text. This phrase storage facility saves keying in time and ensures that spellings are correct. The phrase storage facility may come under a variety of names, such as **abbreviations file, glossary** or **vocabulary store**.
Revision tracking, change bars or change markers	This function offers the ability to produce a printout of a document showing all the changes, amendments and additions that have been made to it during editing. Any deleted words may be shown with a line through them, and any inserted words may be printed out with a line above them. Alternatively, vertical lines may be printed in the margin, called **change bars** or **change markers**, to show the point at which changes have been made. This type of printout enables the author of a document to keep track of any revisions that have been made and to check the amendments without having to proofread the entire text. When the revised draft, marked in this way, has been approved, the operator can print out the final copy with all the amendments carried out. This function is referred to on some systems as the **trace** facility.
Search and replace	A word processing system can search through a document to find a word or words as instructed by the operator. If the operator wishes, the word(s) may then be replaced with different wording on some or all of the occasions it arises. This process is known as **search and replace** or **global search and replace**.
Spelling check	Many word processing systems incorporate a spelling dictionary of 50000 to 100000 words. Documents may be automatically checked for spelling against the words contained in the dictionary. Any words that are incorrectly spelt or that do not appear in the system's dictionary are highlighted so that the typist can correct any spelling mistakes. Systems that include a spelling check function generally allow a limited number of words to be added to the dictionary. A system may also provide for a **personal dictionary** which can contain a limited number of words specific to a particular type of industry or business, such as a chemical industry or an insurance company.
Subscript and superscript	When mathematical or chemical formulae are to be included in a document, the system must be able to print figures or characters above and below the line. **Subscript** characters are printed below the line, as, for example, H_2SO_4. **Superscript** characters are raised above the line, as in $a^2 \times b^3$.

Records processing

Merging text	Variable information can be automatically inserted into a standard letter or other standard document. This variable information may consist of names, addresses, dates, prices, etc. This procedure is often known as the **merging** of standard and variable information.

Selecting

Information may be selected and retrieved from a specially prepared file of details, such as names and addresses, amounts of money, dates, etc. The selection may be made on a single basis, such as the town appearing in the address. Alternatively, selection may be made on the basis of several sets of details, for example, on the basis of those *customers* in a company's *north-west sales region* who owe *more than* £1000 but *less than* £2500.

Sorting

Lists of items, including details, such as names, addresses, dates or figures, that have been keyed into a specially prepared file may be sorted by a word processing system in various ways. They may be automatically re-arranged in alphabetical order, reverse alphabetical order or numerical order. Details may be sorted into subdivided sections. A personnel list may, for example, be sorted to show the names of staff in the order of their joining the firm, under the departments in which they work, the departments being sorted in alphabetical order.

Mathematical functions

Calculations

Some word processing systems include basic arithmetical calculation functions—addition, subtraction, multiplication and division, and possibly the ability to calculate percentages. These arithmetic functions may be applied to text that includes tables of figures, such as invoices, sales reports, time-sheets, etc. The word processor will carry out calculations such as totalling, cross-totalling, averaging, pricing and so on, and insert the figures in the required position.

Programmed key sequences

Some word processors allow the operator to 'program', very simply, a sequence of keystrokes that are required to carry out routine mathematical functions over and over again. The **programmed key sequences** are stored in the system's memory for subsequent recall and use.

This function may be used on statistical tables, where, for example, the operator may regularly need to total several columns, multiply the total of the first column by the total of the second column and insert the final figure in the text. It may also be used to store the sequence of keystrokes needed for the filling in and calculation of invoices.

Communications operations

Communications

Word processors may be able to communicate with other word processors and with various other types of electronic equipment, if they have communications facilities. It is essential that the sending and receiving equipment is **compatible**, which means that they must be able to communicate in the same type of 'electronic language'.

A word processor may be able to send messages to, and receive messages from, word processors, microcomputers, mini- and mainframe computers, Teletex and telex equipment, viewdata and photo-typesetting equipment.

Review questions

1. List the five main areas of operations that can be carried out by word processors.
2. List eight basic text editing functions or operations of a word processor.
3. List six advanced word processing functions.

Activity

Check through the manufacturer's system manual with your teacher and compile a table of the functions available on your system under the five main areas described in Section 5.

SECTION 6   SOME USES OF WORD PROCESSORS

Word processors may be used for **one-off** documents, that is a document which is typed once only, such as a letter or a memo, to produce a perfect copy with no erasures or visible corrections. However, word processing is of greater use for work requiring revision, or which may go through several draft versions before it is produced in its final form. In addition, word processing enables the operator to carry out, at high speeds, selection and sorting procedures ready for the production of a printed document. Some of the functions for which word processing may be useful—in almost any type of company—are listed below.

Circular letters

Many companies send out **circular letters** in which the letter is standard, i.e., the same to every customer, and only the name, address and salutation are different. The system can produce as many letters as required, each one being a top copy and each one addressed to a different person. Lists of names and addresses are stored in a file on the disk. The word processor selects one name and address at a time which it **merges** with the circular letter to produce a personalised letter. In this way, each customer receives a top copy letter with his or her own details printed on it.

A circular letter may need to have several different items of variable information included in it, the details varying from letter to letter. The list of names and addresses can also contain these other details, such as records of a customer's account. As an example, a circular letter may be printed with requests for payment of outstanding accounts, in which case the system can be instructed to select only those customers with overdue accounts.

Forms

Forms may be produced on the word processor. The form may be set up on the screen, with special codes at points where information is to be inserted. The form may then be stored on the disk until required, when the operator will recall the form to the screen, key in the details required and print out the completed form.

Document assembly

Document assembly involves the recording of a series of standard paragraphs and sentences. These standard paragraphs are each given a code and may be recalled to form complete documents. The author selects the paragraphs required from a printed manual in which all available standard paragraphs and their code numbers appear. The word processing operator only needs a list of the required paragraphs plus any new text. These paragraphs are recalled from storage on the disk and printed out, and the completed document has only to be checked for completeness and accuracy of selection, because the text is already known to be correct.

Document assembly, which is sometimes called **boilerplating**, is useful for legal documents such as wills, technical specifications and letters in response to sales enquiries or employment enquiries.

Directories, indexes, stocklists, manuals and handbooks

The internal company telephone directory is a very useful application of word processing, because it often needs up-dating, with changes to staff, departments or telephone numbers. It may be necessary to delete the names of staff who have left or add the names of new staff. When the master copy is stored on disk, it is a simple task to up-date the telephone directory and produce new pages or a complete new copy. Lists of stock, catalogues of products, etc., may be up-dated in the same way. Some word processors are able to sort such lists into various orders, such as alphabetical order, numerical order, order of departments, etc.

Most organisations have manuals of working procedures, handbooks listing induction and training procedures, and manuals giving instructions for the operation of equipment. It is important that they should be kept up to date and this can be done simply by standard editing procedures on the word processor—inserting, deleting and moving text without the need to re-type the whole document. Individual revised pages may be printed out for circulation to holders of the manuals or handbooks for replacement of the out-dated pages.

Personnel records or customer records

Another type of list that may be used on the word processor is the personnel record list, with details of staff such as name, address, age, department and salary. Retrieval of any individual record is very rapid, and when any of the details change, such as the address or salary, it is a simple matter to amend the record of an individual member of staff. Records of a company's customers may also be kept and up-dated in the same way.

Some word processors are able to sort through a list of records and select according to given categories. It may, for example, be desirable to identify all male members of staff who have reached the age of 60 to see whether they would wish to take early retirement, or customers who purchased a particular piece of equipment one year ago may be circularised to remind them that their service agreement is due for renewal.

Progressive documents and financial and statistical documents

Many documents are **progressive**, which means that new items are added and old ones removed over a period of time. A salesman may, for example, keep a list of potential purchasers of the equipment he is selling. When a sale is made, or when it is clear that a particular company is not going to buy the equipment, the names are deleted from the list. As new sales prospects come along, these are added. Financial documents, involving the addition of a month's figures and removal of the same month's figures from the previous year, are also progressive documents. The document can be stored on the disk until the regular amendments to the figures are required. Some word processors can move columns of figures around on statistical documents and some can carry out arithmetic functions, such as adding columns and multiplying items.

Report generation

Several people may be involved in the preparation (or generation) of a report or similar document. One person may prepare a draft of the report and send a copy to several other members of a project team. Each person may then make amendments and additions, which can be incorporated by the word processing operator using standard text editing procedures. A revised draft may then be circulated for further comment. If the appropriate facilities are available, a report may be keyed in to the VDU and transmitted to the VDU of other members of the team without ever being printed out on paper. The authors may discuss the report over the telephone as they view it on the screen and amend the document directly before it is recalled by the original author.

Document revision

As business executives become more accustomed to the new technology, some executives like to make the fullest possible use of the word processing system. The secretary may key in a letter or other document that has been dictated or supplied in manuscript draft form and transmit it to the screen of the VDU on the executive's desk. The executive can then read through the document to ensure that it is ready for final printing, making a few amendments or additions if necessary, and then transmitting the document back to the secretary's VDU for final printing.

List processing or records processing

Some word processing systems can store and manipulate lists of information. These may be, for example, lists of names and addresses but they can be lists of any kind. Special commands are provided to allow the operator to up-date lists, sort through them and extract information. The system may also merge these details with other text for automatic printout of new documents, such as circular letters. This facility to select variable information from a records list file or database and then merge that data into another document is known as **list processing** or **records processing.**

Communications

Many word processing systems are able to provide communications facilities, which are often described as **electronic mailing**. Instead of sending printed copies of memos within a company, for example, the memos may be keyed in by the operator, approved by the author and sent electronically to other work stations. These other work stations may be situated in various offices throughout the building, in different parts of the country or even in another country overseas. At the destination work station, the screen would show that one or more documents were waiting to be viewed and a list of all the electronic mail that had been received could be displayed on the screen. The document selected could be called to the screen and, if required, it could be printed out. However, it might be received by an executive with a terminal on his or her own desk, and after reading it the executive could key in a few words in reply and return it to the originator, without any need ever to print the memo.

Systems such as **Teletex**, the British Telecom electronic mail system, can connect companies on an electronic mail network. External mail in the form of letters, orders and so on can be sent to other companies, as long as they have appropriate and compatible equipment to receive it.

Review questions

1. List five uses of word processing in an organisation.
2. Briefly describe the advantages of keeping personnel records on a word processing system.
3. Briefly describe the way in which a company might use word processors for internal communications.

Activity

Collect samples of circular letters, such as those sent out by mail order companies for advertising purposes, which contain standard and variable information.

SECTION 7   HEALTH AND SAFETY

Health problems may arise for operators working with VDUs, the most common problems being eye fatigue and the fatigue or muscular strain caused by incorrect posture, together with some job stress. There are claims that headaches, neckaches, backaches and eye discomfort are found more frequently among VDU operators than among other office workers. These complaints could be caused by a number of factors, such as poor sitting posture, flickering of the screen, reflections or glare on the screen, or the need for an operator to wear glasses. It is generally possible to eliminate or avoid many of the problems.

Some companies make efforts to reduce the possibilities of such problems by limiting the length of time that an operator will work at the VDU in any day, and they provide a certain number of fixed rest pauses. Other companies ensure that working at a VDU does not make up the whole of any employee's work and design jobs so that working at a word processor is only one of a number of different tasks the employee does during a working day. The general office environment, in terms of furnishings and fittings, is made as pleasant as possible. Some companies arrange for eyesight tests for their staff. Provisions such as these have often been worked out in consultation with trade unions.

All workers who use word processing equipment should be aware of the requirements of the current health and safety legislation, in addition to the specific needs of the VDU operator, which are outlined below.

Ergonomics

The term **ergonomics** is concerned with the study of the relation between the worker, the equipment he or she uses and the working environment. A knowledge of the worker's physical and psychological needs is applied to problems arising from the environment and from the use of equipment. Both manufacturers and purchasers of office equipment are becoming more and more aware of the need to consider ergonomic factors when they design or select equipment. Well-designed equipment can reduce operator fatigue and discomfort.

The screen

A great deal depends on the quality of the character display on the VDU screen. The screen should have a clear, stable image that is easy to read. What is known as the **refresh rate** of the image of the characters on the screen is considered by some people to be of importance to the effects of working at a VDU. The refresh rate refers to a very technical process concerned with the freedom from **flickering** and the length of **after-glow** of the characters on the screen.

The size and shape of the characters on the screen are important. The spacing between characters, between words and between lines should be sufficient to allow both upper and lower case text to be read easily. The colour of the screen is said to have little effect upon the readability of the text compared with the definition of the characters on the screen.

The screen should have a means of adjusting the brightness control and the contrast, and some form of anti-glare protection should be a standard feature of the equipment. Screens that are not provided with anti-reflective surfaces may be improved if a special filter screen is attached to eliminate the glare and reflections that are inevitable in any well-lit office. It is also important to keep the screen clean and dust-free, and this can be done with an anti-static cleaning spray liquid.

Screens should be adjustable, both tilting up and down and rotating from side to side, so that the angle of the screen can be adjusted to suit the operator.

The program

The way in which the word processing program is written affects the operator in terms of fatigue and stress. The type of operator messages provided by the program and the number and complexity of the key operations that have to be entered may make the system easier or more difficult to use. Poorly designed systems can cause frustration for the operator.

The keyboard

The position of the keyboard in relation to the screen, the operator's eyes and the material which is being copied is also an important factor. A keyboard which is separate from the screen and attached only by a length of cable to the VDU will allow the operator to move it to the most convenient and comfortable working position.

The copy

Ideally, the copy from which the operator is working should be placed behind the keyboard on some form of document holder, with the screen slightly to one side. The 'local' lighting falling directly on the copy should be good to help to reduce eye fatigue. Copy-holders are available, designed specially for VDU operators. These sometimes incorporate magnifying devices or a cursor that directs the eyes to the correct line; these can be automatically lowered line by line by means of a foot pedal.

Eyesight

Many people are unaware of their need for spectacles until they start to use a VDU, and problems of eyestrain or eye fatigue, which are blamed on the equipment, may well be indications that the operator is in need of spectacles. People who already wear reading glasses for normal reading distance or for distance vision may find that their spectacles are not appropriate for working at a VDU, if the screen is at a middle distance. Operators who consult an optician for spectacles should mention that they work at a VDU so that the appropriate prescription can be supplied.

Health

A very, very tiny number of people who suffer from a condition known as photosensitive epilepsy may find that working with VDUs is not suitable for them. This condition is *not* caused by VDUs, it is simply one for which medical advice should be sought before undertaking work with a VDU.

Seating

Poor seating can be responsible for much physical fatigue. The height of the chair and the angle and position of the backrest should be adjustable. It is also important that the operator sits correctly on the chair, if muscle strain and fatigue are to be reduced or avoided.

Desking

Specially-designed VDU desks are available, which have split-level surfaces, with the space for the keyboard at the correct height for typing. The desk should be very stable, with enough working surface for the operator to angle the VDU and keyboard at the most comfortable position and to place the copy in an appropriate position.

Noise levels

Printers may be noisy and therefore affect the working conditions of the operator, and add to stress and strain in the working day. Acoustic hoods can be fitted over printers to reduce the noise level, or the printer may be housed in a room separate from the work-stations. Carpeting and curtains, acoustic screen and acoustic ceiling tiles can also reduce noise levels.

Electrical safety

The normal safety precautions taken in connection with electrical equipment in offices should be followed where word processing equipment is concerned. Where a number of work-stations are connected to central resources, there are generally a number of wires and cables making the connections. These should be run through special plastic channelling to ensure that loose wiring does not cause safety hazards.

Review questions

1. In what ways do some companies attempt to reduce the possibilities of health problems for their operators?
2. List the factors concerning the VDU screen that should be considered from the health point of view when selecting a word processing system.
3. What important features should be looked for in a VDU operator's desk and chair?

Activity

Consider your classroom word processing set-up from the health and safety point of view. Prepare a report on the existing conditions, the possible improvements that could be made and the likely costs of such improvements.

PART 2
PRACTICAL UNITS AND ASSIGNMENTS

Starting up the word processor

You are now about to start using the word processor. You should be able to identify the screen, the keyboard, the disk drive and the printer.

Whatever kind of word processing system you use, there will be a **starting-up** operation, in which you will switch on the system and start up the word processing program. If you are using a **shared resource** system, it will most probably be the job of the word processing system manager to start up the system and ensure that the word processing program is in operation ready for use. You will only need to switch on the VDU terminal and **log in** to the system.

If you are using a dedicated word processor or a microcomputer with a word processing program, then you will probably undertake the starting-up procedure yourself. This generally involves at least some, if not all, of the following:

- switching on the electric power;
- switching on the equipment;
- 'booting up' the system with a special initial disk so that it is ready to take the word processing program disk (the system disk);
- inserting the word processing program disk (the system disk) in the drive;
- inserting a working disk in the drive;
- switching on the printer.

Ensure that you are familiar with the start-up routine of your system.

Closing down the system

Ensure also that you are familiar with the close-down routine of your word processing system. This will generally involve some, if not all, of the following:

- 'exiting' from the word processing program;
- when the system instructs you to do so, removing the working disk;
- removing the word processing disk (the system disk);
- if you are using a shared resource system, checking that the other users are ready to switch off;
- switching off the equipment;
- switching off the printer;
- switching off the electric power and removing the plugs from the sockets.

Learning to use a word processor

Learning to use a word processor is quite simple as long as you follow a systematic and logical programme of training. However, one problem is that before you can start to use your word processing system, you need to know how to operate several of the basic functions of the equipment—creating a new document, setting the margins, filing a document, printing, and recalling an existing document for viewing or editing. You need to tackle these basic functions almost at one sitting, which involves taking in a great deal of new information all at once. However, once this has been done it is only a matter of building on this basic knowledge in small, simple steps by learning to use further functions one at a time.

Working the assignments

Each practical unit contains information about one or more word processing functions. You should read through this information carefully so that you understand what word processors in general can do, before you find out how to carry out the functions on your own system.

Your teacher may demonstrate the functions for you and will explain the method to be followed to carry out a particular function on your system. You should make a *brief* note of the method to be followed in the Method Block provided in each unit. This will act as a reminder if you need to refer back to the method of operation at a later stage in the course. You may also make a note of the page on which the function is explained fully in the system manual. An example of a completed Method Block is shown in Fig. P1.

Figure P1 A completed Method Block

METHOD	Write in the space provided below a brief note of the method used on your system, and see Page(s) ......10 and 11.......................... of your system manual.
CREATE A DOCUMENT	Call up the main menu. Place cursor against DRAFT on the list of options. Press the EXECUTE key. Wait for instruction to appear in the operator instruction line. Key in the name of the document in the operator instruction line. Press the EXECUTE key.

When you know how to carry out the necessary functions on your word processor, you are ready to work the assignment related to that function. Each unit contains one or more assignments based on the functions already learnt, and all the assignments are concerned with a company called Zocar Word and Data Processing Limited.

Follow the instructions given on the Word Processing Request Form given for each assignment. Be sure to read the instructions carefully. When you are asked to CREATE a new document, the instructions on the Word Processing Request Form will give you the name you are to use for the document you create. You should add your initials to the document name for each assignment, so that you will be able to identify your own documents. The first assignment is called **spray/your initials** (for example, **spray/dcm**).

When you have set the margins and the page format, the first items to be keyed in to the document are the assignment number and your name. If you share a printer, this will ensure that you can identify your own document when it is printed out.

You will notice that Assignment 1 is not to be corrected or printed out. However, for all other assignments, you should always carry out the following proofreading and checking routine before printing the document.

When you have finished keying in the document, proofread and check it on the screen. Print out the document. Proofread the printed document. If you find one or more errors, recall the document to the screen, correct the mistakes and print out a correct copy. When you are satisfied that your work is correct, take it to your teacher for assessment.

Remember—it is your responsibility to ensure that your work is accurate and correct.

A Personal Record Log Sheet is printed on page 129. You can use this to record the time you spend operating the word processing system. Record the date, the time (to the nearest quarter-hour) and the functions covered, in the spaces provided. The total time you spend on 'hands-on' practical operation of the system can be recorded on the Word Processing Certificate of Competence you will produce as Assignment 25—the last assignment.

UNIT 1

**CREATE A NEW DOCUMENT
SET LEFT AND RIGHT MARGINS
TOP MARGIN • WORD WRAP
FILE A DOCUMENT**

Creating or drafting a document

One of the first things you need to learn to do is to create or draft a document. A document is simply what you would call a page (or several pages) of typed work. Different systems use different names for the same functions, and making a new document may be called **create** or **draft**—or some other name. The term **create** will be used in this book.

In order to create a new document, the word processing system must be given a set of instructions. These instructions may be given by means of commands selected from the menu, if the system is menu-based. Alternatively, the instructions for creating or drafting a new document may be given by means of the status line or command line, where a series of questions may be presented and the answers keyed in by the operator. Whatever the method used on any particular system, the following information is generally required as a minimum.

The system must be told that you wish to create, or draft, a new document. This may, for example, require the keying in of the character C, or perhaps pressing a key marked CREATE or DRAFT.

You must key in a name for the document you are going to create. The name allocated should give some guidance as to the contents of the document, so that when you wish to refer to the list of stored documents on the index you can identify them easily. On most systems it will then be necessary to press an EXECUTE or ACTION key to tell the system to carry out the instruction to create the document. You must then give the system information about the way in which your page of text is to be displayed, or laid out, before you start to key in text. These layout requirements are usually called the **format** of the document.

Format or layout of the document

Page format or layout is basically concerned with the setting of margins, tabs, line spacing, page length, pitch (size of type) and other items that affect the way in which the text is laid out on the page. You will start by learning how to set the basic format requirements.

The point in the production of a document at which instructions are given to the system concerning format requirements varies from system to system. They may all be set on a ruler or format line before the document is keyed in. Alternatively some items, such as margins and tabs, may be set on a ruler or format line before the document is keyed in, while other commands concerning line spacing, pitch, page length, etc, may be set on a print format or print menu after the document has been keyed in but before it is printed.

Whatever the stage of the operation at which the format is specified, all systems must be given these instructions in one form or another before a document is printed out.

The format may be changed at any point while a document is being keyed in or when it is later being edited, and several formats may be used within one document by inserting rulers or format lines at desired positions to change the margins, line spacing, pitch or tab stop positions.

Setting left and right margins

Most systems have a **default margin** which provides margin settings if the operator fails to set them. However, the margins may be set as desired in place of the default settings.

The names for margin-setting lines vary from system to system, but common terms are **format lines** or **rulers**. The term **ruler** will be used in this book. The ruler may be permanently displayed at the top of the screen. Alternatively, the information concerning margin settings may be included on the operator information line or status line if there is one.

Many systems allow the operator to store margin settings that are frequently used, in order to save time. When a standard margin setting is likely to be required frequently the operator will store, or save, the setting so that it can later be recalled on command.

The left margin is set by giving the system the appropriate instruction, which may be, for example, keying in L for the left margin at the desired position.

On most systems two or three types of right margin may generally be set: ragged, semi-justified and justified. A **ragged margin** is the normal uneven right margin, as on work produced on a traditional typewriter. A **semi-justified right margin** is one in which extra spacing is distributed evenly along the lines of type so that the right margin is tidier than a ragged margin but is not fully justified. A **justified right margin** is one in which extra spacing is distributed evenly along the lines of type so that the last character of every line falls at the same point resulting in a completely even right margin.

Top margin

On most word processors a top margin of 1 inch (25 mm) is automatically allowed for by the system, and when you print out a document the printer will turn up six or seven line spaces before starting to print.

If you need to place a short piece of text fairly centrally down the page, it is *not* good practice to insert a large number of extra clear line spaces at the top of the document when it is being keyed in. Each clear line space will take up storage space in the memory of the word processor, and this wastes space on the disk. If you are printing out a short document you may turn the paper through the printer an extra inch or two, as required, so that the text is printed fairly centrally on the paper. Some word processors, however, do have a function for centring text vertically on the page. If your system is able to do this, then you should learn to use the function.

Typing in wraparound, or word wrap

Remember that once the right margin has been set on the ruler line you do not need to worry about the length of the typing line—the system will decide when it has enough words on a line and will wrap the following word onto the next line. You will only type in a **hard return** using the RETURN key at such points as the end of a heading, at the end of a paragraph, at the end of each line in a tabulated statement or where an extra clear line space is required.

Line spacing

The line spacing on the word processor is automatically set at single line spacing. This may be changed to $1\frac{1}{2}$, double, $2\frac{1}{2}$ and treble line spacing. Your first assignments will be in single line spacing.

Filing or storing a document

When a document has been created you may wish to keep it on file in the storage system of the word processor, so that you may refer to it again and, if necessary, edit or change it in some way. With many systems it is necessary to file the document by giving the system a command or a series of commands. On other systems a document is filed automatically.

ASSIGNMENT NO 1

METHOD	Write in the space provided below a brief note of the method used on your system, and see Page(s) .... of your system manual.
CREATE A DOCUMENT	
SET MARGINS - left margin - right margin	
FILE A DOCUMENT	

ZOCAR WORD AND DATA PROCESSING LIMITED – WORD PROCESSING REQUEST FORM   ASSIGNMENT NO _1_

CREATE a new document ..✓..		New document to be named spray/your initials	
EDIT an existing document		Existing document named	
LEFT MARGIN AT ..25.. RIGHT MARGIN AT ..75..		Right margin to be – Ragged ..✓.. Justified	
LINE SPACING	PITCH	PAPER	NO OF COPIES REQUIRED
1 ..✓.. 1½ ..... 2 ..... AND/OR as shown on draft	12 ..✓.. 10	Plain A4 ..✓.. Headed A4	~~Print ...... copy(ies)~~ DO **NOT** PRINT A COPY
FILING INSTRUCTIONS – RETAIN document on file ..✓.. DELETE document from file			

SPECIAL INSTRUCTIONS

Do **NOT** correct any errors you make as you key in the document on this first Assignment. Leave the errors so that you can correct them in Assignment 3, which deals with editing a document.

At the top of the document, key in

    Assignments 1 and 2
    Your name

Press the RETURN key <u>ONCE</u> after the Assignment number, <u>FOUR TIMES</u> after your name, and <u>TWICE</u> after each heading.

When you are keying in the paragraphs, remember that you <u>DO NOT</u> press the RETURN key at the end of a line. The system will decide on line endings for you with the word wrap facility.

At the <u>end</u> of each paragraph, press the RETURN key <u>twice</u>.

Assignments 1 and 2
(Your name)

ZOCAR WORD AND DATA PROCESSING LIMITED

ZOCAR ANTI-STATIC SPRAY

Are you aware of the need to protect your visual display units against static electricity? A build-up of static electricity can cause problems in your word processing terminals.

Now you can protect your valuable equipment with a spray can of Zocar Anti-static Spray. The spray cans are simple to use and easy to carry.

A 450 g aerosol can will cost you only £6.00. Buy one for each work station and benefit from our special offer of 5 cans for only £27.50.

UNIT 2

PRINTING A DOCUMENT
PROOFREADING AND PROOF CORRECTION

Printing a document

The routine to be followed by the operator in order to print a document varies from system to system, and the number and type of instructions to be given to the word processor also vary. With some systems it is possible to print direct from the screen, but with many word processors it is necessary to file the document before it can be printed.

Before a copy is printed out, the system must be given information concerning the paper size, the number of copies required, the size of type to be used and various other details. These details concerning printing will vary from machine to machine. In some cases, for example, the 'name' of the printer to be used must be identified.

Proofreading

When you have keyed in a document you should carefully proofread and check the text on the screen and correct any errors you may find. Time and energy can be wasted if errors are found after the document has been printed out, as it will be necessary to recall the document, make the required alterations and print out another copy.

Unless you are given other instructions, you should remember that it is *your* responsibility to proofread and check all work you do on the word processor, both on the screen *and* after printing it out, comparing it carefully with the original draft and with the instructions given on the Word Processing Request Form.

A list of commonly used proof correction signs is shown on the next page. Use these correction signs when you are proofreading a printed copy, marking each correction with a coloured pen in order to identify it clearly, ready for screen editing.

Proof correction signs

The following corrections should be used when proofreading and correcting printed copy. The appropriate sign should be written in the margin and the text marked as shown in the EXAMPLE column.

SIGN	MEANING	EXAMPLE
⋏	Insert a character, word, etc	Pr⋏nt a copy⋏me⋏please. (i, for, ,)
⊤ (with loop)	Insert a character, word, etc	It is⋏done and⋏sent off. (now, ready to be)
#	Insert a space	# Take the⋏package today.
⌒	Close up a space	My or⌒der is ⌒ready.
CAPS	Use capitals	(Information Pack) CAPS
u.c.	Use capitals where indicated	u.c. information folder
SP. CAPS	Use spaced capitals	(Word Processing) SP. CAPS
l.c.	Use lower case letters	l.c. The Committee Meeting
u/sc	Underline as indicated	u/sc Word Processing Centre
NP [	Begin a new paragraph where indicated by square bracket	We can do that for you NP today. [Let us know if you are ready for it.
//	Begin a new paragraph where indicated by the double oblique lines	Please send it as soon as possible.// Our new Bristol office is ready for it.
⟿	Run on - do not start a new paragraph	Thank you for your letter of 15 January.⟿ run on ⟨We received it today.
stet	Let the original stand - type the word or words with the dotted line underneath, even though crossed out.	stet This was ~~provided~~ for our stet ~~employees~~ ~~workers~~ in the past. (given)
trs ⌒⌒	Transpose - change the order as shown	trs Change two letter(s r) or trs change one or (words more).

WORD PROCESSING—SYSTEMS, APPLICATIONS AND ASSIGNMENTS

ASSIGNMENT NO 2

METHOD	Write in the space provided below a brief note of the method used on your system, and see Page(s) .... of your system manual.
PRINT A DOCUMENT	

ZOCAR WORD AND DATA PROCESSING LIMITED – WORD PROCESSING REQUEST FORM ASSIGNMENT NO 2

~~CREATE a new document~~ ..... New document to be named ....
~~EDIT an existing document~~ ..... Existing document named **spray/your initials**
LEFT MARGIN AT ...2.5... RIGHT MARGIN AT ...7.5... Right margin to be – Ragged ..✓.... Justified ....

LINE SPACING	PITCH	PAPER	NO OF COPIES REQUIRED
1 ..✓.. 1½ ..... 2 ..... AND/OR as shown on draft	12 ..✓... 10	Plain A4 ..✓.... Headed A4	Print ...1... copy~~(ies)~~

FILING INSTRUCTIONS – RETAIN document on file ..✓.... DELETE document from file ......
SPECIAL INSTRUCTIONS For this Assignment you will print out the document named spray/your initials ready for proofreading. When you keyed in Assignment 1 you were instructed not to correct any errors you made. On your printed copy, identify the errors (if any) in need of correction by marking them with a coloured pen, using the proof correction signs — ready for editing the text in Assignment 3.

UNIT 3

CHECK INDEX
RECALL/EDIT A DOCUMENT
CURSOR MOVEMENT • INSERT TEXT
DELETE TEXT

The index of documents

Every document that is created and filed is automatically listed by the system on the index of documents. Some systems arrange all documents in alphabetical order so that tracing a document is made easier. A number may be automatically allocated to the document in addition to the name given by the operator.

When you wish to find a particular document you can check that it is stored on the disk by calling up the index or directory. On many systems this is done by selecting the index option from the menu. Check that you have the *exact* document name for the document you wish to look at. It is important on some systems that upper and lower case characters are exactly as shown on the index, otherwise the system will not recognise that the name you key in is the same as the name listed in the index. This is known as being **case sensitive**, that is, the system is **sensitive** to whether the name has been keyed in in upper or lower case.

Recalling an existing document for editing

You have created a document called **spray/your initials** and filed it, so that it is now listed on the index and stored on disk ready to be recalled when you want to look at it or alter it in any way.

When you make any alterations or amendments to a document on the screen this is known as **editing** the document. Even if you only wish to recall the document to the screen so that you can look at it, without making any amendments, you will use the **edit** function.

If you wish to recall your document to the screen, you must give the system the appropriate instructions. This may be done on some systems by selecting an **edit** or **recall** function from the menu, or on other systems by pressing a code key and a character such as E followed by an EXECUTE or ACTION key. The document will then be displayed on the screen.

Moving the cursor about the screen

An important aspect of keying in and editing text is the speedy and efficient use of the cursor movement keys. You need to know how to move the cursor around the screen rapidly using the most appropriate cursor movement function.

On the majority of word processors special cursor movement keys are marked with directional arrows, which indicate that the cursor may be moved right, left, up or down. Even if there are no special directional arrow keys on your system, there will be some means of moving the cursor right, left, up or down. Using these keys, the cursor may be moved one space at a time in the direction indicated, and you should use these keys where only small movements are required. The cursor may also be moved forward word by word, by line, sentence or paragraph, and backwards by word, line, sentence or paragraph. There is usually also some method of moving the cursor directly to the start of the document and the end of the document.

These cursor facilities provide for rapid movement around the screen, and you should practise until you can quickly select the most appropriate way of moving the cursor directly to the position you want when editing text.

Inserting text

Word processors may operate either in **insert mode** or in **overtype mode**—or it may be possible to switch from one mode to the other on the same system. In either case, if you wish to insert a character, a word or a larger amount of text, the cursor is moved to the position at which the new character, or the first character of the new text, is to be inserted.

On a word processor that operates in **insert mode** the new character or word to be inserted is keyed in, and the system 'pushes' the remaining text along to make room for it, at the same time adjusting the length of each following line with the word wrap facility.

On a word processor that operates in **overtype mode**, the appropriate key or keys must be pressed to tell the system that new text is to be inserted. Many systems then highlight the point at which the text is to be inserted, or may cause a break in the text by dropping the next portion of text down the screen to the next line. The new text is then keyed in, and the appropriate key pressed to instruct the system to go back to overtype mode when the text is joined up to the newly inserted text.

Deleting text

Most word processors can delete text in one of two ways—either backwards or forwards. When you are editing text that has already been keyed in, you are more likely to use the **forwards delete function key**, because you will move the cursor to the first of the characters to be deleted and delete forwards one space. Some systems may also have a function that will delete forwards a word at a time, or a sentence, line, paragraph or even page at a time. These functions must be used with care to ensure that only unwanted text is deleted.

When you are keying in text you are more likely to use the **backwards delete function key**, because as soon as you realise you have made an error you will wish to 'backspace' over the error to delete it and re-key the correct characters or words. The backwards delete function key will move the cursor backwards deleting one character at a time. Some systems may, in addition, have a key that will delete backwards a whole word or a whole sentence at a time.

If you wish to correct an error as you are keying in text, the method may vary depending on the type of system you are using. On a word processor that operates in insert mode, the incorrect character or characters are generally deleted backwards as soon as you realise you have made a mistake, and the correct characters keyed in. However, on some word processing systems that operate in overtype mode, the operator will simply move the cursor to the point at which the error has occurred and overtype the incorrect characters with the correct ones.

ASSIGNMENT NO 3

METHOD	Write in the space provided below a brief note of the method used on your system, and see Page(s) .... of your system manual.
CHECK INDEX	
RECALL A DOCUMENT	
MOVING THE CURSOR	
INSERT TEXT	
DELETE TEXT	

ZOCAR WORD AND DATA PROCESSING LIMITED - WORD PROCESSING REQUEST FORM ASSIGNMENT NO 3

CREATE a new document	New document to be named ....
EDIT an existing document ..✓..	Existing document named **spray/your initials**
LEFT MARGIN AT ..25.. RIGHT MARGIN AT ..75..	Right margin to be - Ragged ..✓.. Justified ....

LINE SPACING	PITCH	PAPER	NO OF COPIES REQUIRED
1 ..✓.. 1½ ..... 2 ..... AND/OR as shown on draft	12 ..✓.. 10	Plain A4 ..✓.. Headed A4	Print ..1.. copy(~~ies~~)

FILING INSTRUCTIONS - RETAIN document on file ..✓.. DELETE document from file ......

SPECIAL INSTRUCTIONS

1. Practise moving the cursor around the screen, using all the cursor movement functions.

2. Change the Assignment number to Assignment 3.

3. Correct any errors you made when keying in the document, using the DELETE and INSERT functions.

4. Make the amendments shown on the Assignment by deleting and inserting text as necessary.

Assignment 3
(Your name)

ZOCAR WORD AND DATA PROCESSING LIMITED

ZOCAR ANTI-STATIC SPRAY

Are you aware of the need to protect your visual display units against static electricity? Do you know that a build-up of static electricity can cause problems in your word processing terminals.

Now you can protect your ~~valuable~~ equipment with a spray can of Zocar Anti-static Spray. ~~The spray cans are simple to use and easy to carry.~~

A 450 g aerosol can of Zocar Anti-Static Spray will cost you only £6.00. Buy one for each work station and benefit from our special offer of 5 cans for only £27.50.

UNIT 4

CHANGE MARGINS • CHANGE LINE SPACING
MAKE A NEW PARAGRAPH
RUN TWO PARAGRAPHS INTO ONE

Re-formatting text

You have now created, filed, recalled, edited and printed a document.

The document can now be recalled again so that the format can be changed. In other words, the document will be **re-formatted**.

As described on page 43 several items are involved in the format of a document—the margins, line spacing, the size of type and so on. In this unit, you will change only the line spacing and margins.

On many word processing systems the text may still appear *on the screen* in single line spacing even though you have given instructions to the system to *print* the document in double line spacing. The instruction to change from single to double line spacing will be carried out only when the document is actually printed.

ASSIGNMENT NO 4

METHOD	Write in the space provided below a brief note of the method used on your system, and see Page(s) .... of your system manual.
CHANGE MARGINS	
CHANGE LINE SPACING	
MAKE A NEW PARAGRAPH	
RUN TWO PARAGRAPHS INTO ONE	

ZOCAR WORD AND DATA PROCESSING LIMITED – WORD PROCESSING REQUEST FORM   ASSIGNMENT NO 4

CREATE a new document	New document to be named ....
EDIT an existing document ✓....	Existing document named **spray/your initials**

LEFT MARGIN AT ...**18**....
RIGHT MARGIN AT ...**78**....   Right margin to be – Ragged ..✓.... Justified ....

LINE SPACING	PITCH	PAPER	NO OF COPIES REQUIRED
1 ..... 1½ ..... 2 ✓..... AND/OR as shown on draft	12 ✓.... 10	Plain A4 ✓.... Headed A4	Print ...**1**.... copy(~~ies~~)

FILING INSTRUCTIONS – RETAIN document on file ✓..... DELETE document from file ......

SPECIAL INSTRUCTIONS

WORD PROCESSING—SYSTEMS, APPLICATIONS AND ASSIGNMENTS

Assignment 4
(Your name)

ZOCAR WORD AND DATA PROCESSING LIMITED

ZOCAR ANTI-STATIC SPRAY

Are you aware of the ~~need to~~ *importance of* protect*ing* your visual display units against static electricity? Do you know that a build-up of static electricity can cause problems in your word processing terminals? *run on* Now you can protect your equipment with a spray can of Zocar Anti-static Spray.

A 450 g aerosol can of Zocar Anti-static Spray will cost you only £6.00. *NP* Buy one for each work station and benefit from our special offer of 5 cans for only £27.50.

Write for our free full-colour brochure of office supplies.

UNIT 5

JUSTIFIED RIGHT MARGIN
DELETING A DOCUMENT FROM THE FILE

Justified right margin

As described on page 44, word processors can print a document with a completely even right margin, with every line of text ending at the same point. Extra white space is automatically inserted along the lines of text, either between words or on some systems between characters as well as between words. On some word processors the justification of the right margin is not shown on the screen, and the text is justified only when the document is printed out. On many systems, however, the operator can view the justified text on the screen before printing out, and this is obviously a great advantage for the operator.

The point at which the system is given the instruction to justify the right margin varies and your system may operate in one of the following ways:

1. At the margin setting stage, the operator instructs the system to print with a justified right margin by, for example, keying in a J for the right margin setting.
2. The instruction may be given to the system when the word processor is being given commands for printing.
3. The process of justifying text may be carried out after text has been keyed in but before printing out. The operator presses the appropriate command keys and instructs the system to justify the right margin of the text. The system asks the operator to highlight, or identify, the paragraphs which are to be justified, and a further command causes the system to carry out the justification process. This particular method is very flexible, because it allows individual paragraphs within a document to be justified without the need to set additional ruler or format lines.

Deleting a document from the file

When a document has been created, printed out and approved, a decision has to be made as to whether that document will be kept on the files of the system or, in other words, whether it is going to be allowed to take up storage space on the disk. If every document were kept, a great deal of space on the disks would be taken up unnecessarily, and therefore wasted.

The job of deleting, or clearing off, unwanted documents is an important part of what is known as **housekeeping**. Only those documents that may need to be referred to again for printing or editing should be retained on the files on disk.

The system is given an instruction to delete a document, either through selecting the DELETE option from a menu, or through a sequence of keystrokes. Most systems operate a **double check procedure**, which gives the operator the opportunity to confirm that a particular document is to be deleted. For example, the system may provide an operator prompt that asks 'Are you sure you want to delete document 'spray/dcm'?' The operator then has the opportunity to cancel the DELETE command or to confirm that the deletion of the document from the file should take place.

Once a document has been deleted from the disk, it is not possible (on many systems) to recall it, and if it were needed again the operator would have to key it in to the system again. However, there are some systems which operate on a **waste-bin** approach. Deleted documents may be held in memory in the waste-bin for a specified period, perhaps 12 hours, and in that time the operator may retrieve deleted documents just as you might retrieve a typed document from the waste paper basket.

Because deletion of documents from the files is permanent, it is important that they should only be deleted when it is certain that there is no further value in keeping them on disk. In an office, the decision about whether to retain or keep a document on the files will be taken by the word processing supervisor together with the author of the document, in accordance with company policy. The operator should only delete documents if instructions are given to do so, otherwise valuable time may have to be spent keying in and checking the text again.

When you are working through the practical assignments in this book, you will be given instructions on the Word Processing Request Form about retaining (keeping) your documents on file or deleting them. Even when you are given instructions to delete a document from the file, do be careful *not* to do so until your teacher has approved and assessed your work.

ASSIGNMENT NO 5

METHOD	Write in the space provided below a brief note of the method used on your system, and see Page(s) .... of your system manual.
JUSTIFIED RIGHT MARGIN DELETE A DOCUMENT FROM FILE	

ZOCAR WORD AND DATA PROCESSING LIMITED – WORD PROCESSING REQUEST FORM   ASSIGNMENT NO 5

CREATE a new document	New document to be named ....
EDIT an existing document ..✓..	Existing document named **spray/your initials**

LEFT MARGIN AT ...**20**... RIGHT MARGIN AT ...**79**...		Right margin to be – Ragged .... Justified ..✓..	
LINE SPACING	PITCH	PAPER	NO OF COPIES REQUIRED
1 ..... 1½ ..✓.. 2 ..... AND/OR as shown on draft	12 ..✓.. 10	Plain A4 ..✓.. Headed A4	Print ..**1**.. copy(~~ies~~)
FILING INSTRUCTIONS – RETAIN document on file ...... DELETE document from file ..✓..			
SPECIAL INSTRUCTIONS			

Assignment 5

(Your name)

ZOCAR WORD AND DATA PROCESSING LIMITED

ZOCAR ANTI-STATIC SPRAY

Are you aware of the importance of protecting your visual display units against static electricity? Do you know that a build-up of static electricity can cause problems in your word processing terminals? [NP] Now you can protect your equipment with a spray can of Zocar Anti-static Spray. [run on]

A 450 g aerosol can of Zocar Anti-static Spray will cost you only £6.00. [run on]

Buy one for each work station and benefit from our special offer of 5 cans for only £27.50.

To get a copy of ~~Write for~~ our free full-colour brochure of office supplies, just complete the enclosed reply-paid card and post it to Zocar Word and Data Processing Limited — or simply telephone our Supplies Department on (0704) 393935.

UNIT 6

INSERTING ADDITIONAL RULERS IN TEXT TO CHANGE MARGINS AND LINE SPACING

Additional rulers or format lines may be set at any point in a document, so that two or more styles of layout can be included within one document. The extra rulers or format lines may be inserted either while you are keying in the document or inserted in existing text when you are carrying out editing work.

When you are drafting or creating a document, you may wish to inset text from the left and right margins, or change the line spacing within the document. This may be done in various ways, but one method is through the insertion of additional rulers or format lines in the text, as described above. The margins and line spacing can be changed from the point where a new ruler line is inserted.

Once a new ruler or format line has been inserted in the text it will affect all the following text until another ruler is inserted to change back to the original layout or to provide yet a further change of margins and/or line spacing.

Word processors are very sophisticated machines, and there are often at least two ways of achieving the layout you want. The good operator is able to make the most appropriate choice of function for the particular work in hand. It is possible, for example, to inset text from the left and/or right margins by using the indent function where this is available on the system. Bear in mind that the function being learnt at the moment concerns changing margins and line spacing by inserting additional rulers or format lines. If your word processing system provides for this function, then use it for the assignments that follow. If your system does not allow for the insertion of additional ruler lines, then use the method available on your system to adjust the margins and line spacing as shown in the assignments.

You will need to take some care with the line spacing between paragraphs when you are changing from double line spacing to single line spacing. Unless you are using a word processing system that shows on the screen exactly what the document will look like when it is printed out, it takes a little time to get used to visualising what the finished text will look like.

Until you have gained a little more experience with your system, you may need to print out a draft copy of your document to see what has happened to the line spacing. If the line spacing is not correct, you can recall the document and delete or insert line spacing as necessary, and then print out your final copy.

ASSIGNMENT NO 6

METHOD	Write in the space provided below a brief note of the method used on your system, and see Page(s) .... of your system manual.
INSERT ADDITIONAL RULERS IN TEXT TO CHANGE MARGINS AND LINE SPACING	

ZOCAR WORD AND DATA PROCESSING LIMITED – WORD PROCESSING REQUEST FORM   ASSIGNMENT NO 6

CREATE a new document ✓   New document to be named **brochure/your initials**

EDIT an existing document .....   Existing document named ....

LEFT MARGIN AT **20**
RIGHT MARGIN AT **79**   Right margin to be – Ragged ✓   Justified ......
and as shown on draft

LINE SPACING	PITCH	PAPER	NO OF COPIES REQUIRED
1 ..... 1½ ..... 2 ✓	12 ✓	Plain A4 ✓	Print **1** copy~~(ies)~~
AND/~~OR~~ as shown on draft ✓	10	Headed A4	

FILING INSTRUCTIONS – RETAIN document on file ......   DELETE document from file ✓

SPECIAL INSTRUCTIONS

UNIT 6

> **OPERATOR**
> Left margin 20, Right margin 79, Double line spacing

Assignment 6

(Your name)

ZOCAR WORD AND DATA PROCESSING LIMITED

Here is your opportunity to browse through a selection of today's most advanced business products, and at the same time take advantage of the expertise and personal service for which Zocar Word and Data Processing Limited are famous.

> **OPERATOR:** New ruler line here: LM30, RM70, Single line spacing

Every Zocar product is covered by our own quality guarantee, and our nation-wide servicing ~~ensures that you have~~ assures you of prompt, reliable after-sales service at all times.

> **OPERATOR:** New ruler line here: LM20, RM79, Double line spacing

Use the order form enclosed with our brochure, or, if you prefer, telephone our Supplies Department. Our sales staff are waiting to help you.

If you are near one of our stores, ~~why not~~ you are welcome to step in to see the wide range and high quality of our products.

> **OPERATOR:** New ruler line here: LM20, RM79, Single line spacing

ZOCAR WORD AND DATA PROCESSING LIMITED
1 Exhibition Square
SOUTHPORT
Merseyside
PR9 2EG

Telephone (0704) 393935

UNIT 7

CENTRING LINES OF TEXT
VIEWING SERVICE CODES

Centring lines of text

Almost all word processing systems will centre headings or other single items of text. The heading or item to be centred is generally typed at the left margin, and the appropriate commands are given to the system instructing it to centre the item. The line of text will automatically be centred between the margins that have been set. If the items are to be centred accurately across the page, as well as over the text, then it is necessary to ensure that the left and right margins are equal.

Most word processors will actually move the line of text and show the item centred on the screen as it will appear when the document is printed out. However, on some less sophisticated systems, the line of text will remain at the left margin on the screen, even though the system has accepted the command to print it as centred, and the centring will only take place when the document is printed out.

If centring does not show on the screen, it is usually possible to give a command to enable you to see or **view** the text together with what are known as service codes. The system will show on the screen a symbol which indicates to the operator that the item will be centred when it is printed out.

Viewing service codes

As described above, it is sometimes necessary to see or view the service codes as well as the actual text that will be printed out. These codes have different names on various systems—on some systems, for example, they are known as the **trace codes**. There will usually be a dot to represent each blank character space, for example, and other symbols will represent rulers, format lines, tab stops, centring, etc.

The service codes may be visible at all times on the screen display, together with the text. Alternatively, it may be necessary on some systems to call up the codes by pressing one or more keys to view them. On other systems certain of the codes, such as a hard return at the end of a paragraph or a clear line space, will always be visible with the text, and others will be seen only when the operator wishes to view them, which can be done by pressing the appropriate command keys.

When the text is displayed together with these service codes it is possible to identify all the functions that have been carried out by the system. These service codes are very useful, therefore, when the operator is editing text and wants to discover the position of commands. They are also helpful when setting up a complicated piece of work such as an organisation chart or tabular statement. In addition, they can be useful to an experienced operator for 'diagnostic purposes' if a problem arises when re-formatting text. The service codes help the operator to diagnose, or find out, what is going wrong by identifying what functions have been carried out on the text.

If your word processor has this facility for viewing the service codes, use it to examine and identify the codes when you have finished inputting the text for Assignment 7. Use the system manual to help you identify the various symbols that represent functions such as character space and centring.

ASSIGNMENT NO 7

METHOD	Write in the space provided below a brief note of the method used on your system, and see Page(s) .... of your system manual.
CENTRING LINES OF TEXT	
VIEWING SERVICE CODES	

ZOCAR WORD AND DATA PROCESSING LIMITED - WORD PROCESSING REQUEST FORM   ASSIGNMENT NO 7

CREATE a new document ..✓.. New document to be named **orders/your initials**
EDIT an existing document ..... Existing document named ....
LEFT MARGIN AT ...**22**........ RIGHT MARGIN AT ...**78**........ Right margin to be - Ragged .... Justified ..✓.. **AND as shown on draft**

LINE SPACING	PITCH	PAPER	NO OF COPIES REQUIRED
1 ..✓... 1½ ..... 2 ..... AND/~~OR~~ as shown on draft ✓..	12 ✓.... 10	Plain A4 ..✓.. Headed A4	Print ..**1**.. copy~~(ies)~~

FILING INSTRUCTIONS - RETAIN document on file ...... DELETE document from file ✓..
SPECIAL INSTRUCTIONS

UNIT 7

OPERATOR: Left margin 22, Right margin 78, Single line spacing

Assignment 7
(Your name)

ZOCAR WORD AND DATA PROCESSING LIMITED — centre

We hope you find our new brochure informative and interesting, and that you are now ready to order your word and data processing supplies from our extensive range.

There are two ways to order goods. You can either post the order form to us or telephone us.

OPERATOR: INSERT NEW RULER LINE HERE: LM 32, RM 68, 1½ line spacing

USING THE ORDER FORM — centre

If you use the order form, please complete all details in BLOCK CAPITALS and post it to us in the FREEPOST envelope supplied with the brochure.

ORDERING BY TELEPHONE — centre

To order by telephone, call our Supplies Department, where our ~~helpful~~ sales staff will be ready to record your requirements. [STET]

OPERATOR: INSERT NEW RULER LINE HERE. LM 22, RM 78, Single line spacing

You may pay by cheque or use your credit card. Simply write your card number in the space provided, add your signature, and include the expiry date of your card. If you are ordering by telephone, simply give this information over the telephone to our sales staff. Our telephone number is:

SOUTHPORT (0704) 393935 — centre

UNIT 8

CENTRING BLOCKS OF TEXT

Centring blocks of text

In addition to centring a single line of text such as a heading, many word processors can also centre whole blocks of text. The operator presses the appropriate keys to instruct the system to perform the centring function. The system responds by printing a message on the screen asking the operator to define, or 'show' the word processor, the quantity of text to be centred. The operator defines the text that is to be centred by moving the cursor from the starting point of the block of text to be centred to the end of the block of text.

The text that has been defined in this way is usually highlighted, often by **reverse** or **inverse video**, which means that the colour of the characters and screen are reversed. When the quantity of text has been defined, the command sequence is continued by pressing the appropriate keys to instruct the system to carry out the centring operation.

This block centring function is very useful and time-saving. When you carry out the assignments you should key in the whole block of text that is to be centred and then carry out the centring function on the block. If, however, your word processor does not have the facility to centre blocks of text, you will have to centre individual lines as you key them in.

ASSIGNMENT NO 8

METHOD	Write in the space provided below a brief note of the method used on your system, and see Page(s) .... of your system manual.
CENTRE BLOCKS OF TEXT	

ZOCAR WORD AND DATA PROCESSING LIMITED – WORD PROCESSING REQUEST FORM   ASSIGNMENT NO 8

CREATE a new document ..✓... New document to be named ...*leaflet/your initials*........
EDIT an existing document ..... Existing document named ....
LEFT MARGIN AT ...20.......   RIGHT MARGIN AT ...79....... Right margin to be – Ragged .... Justified ..✓...

LINE SPACING	PITCH	PAPER	NO OF COPIES REQUIRED
1 ..✓... 1½ ..... 2 ..... AND/OR as shown on draft	12 ..✓... 10	Plain A4 ..✓... Headed A4	Print ..1... copy(~~ies~~)

FILING INSTRUCTIONS – RETAIN document on file ...... DELETE document from file ..✓...
SPECIAL INSTRUCTIONS

Assignment 8
(Your name)

ZOCAR WORD AND DATA PROCESSING LIMITED — centre

We offer the fastest and most economical delivery service in the country, the most efficient back-up service and the highest quality products. Not only can we provide all your data processing and word processing supplies, but the order you place today will be in your office the next working day in most parts of the country.

Continuous Stationery
Floppy Disks
Printer Ribbons
Acoustic Hoods
Magnetic Tape
Daisy Wheels
~~Printer Ribbons~~
Diskette Storage
Printout Filing and Storage
Microfiche and Storage
Tape and Disk Storage

— centre each line of this block of text

We are convinced you will be impressed with the quality of our products, but if you are not completely satisfied we will refund your money in full. We give a 12 month guarantee with every product we provide. You can rely on Zocar.

ZOCAR WORD AND DATA PROCESSING LIMITED
1 Exhibition Square
SOUTHPORT
Merseyside
PR9 2EG

Telephone (0704) 393935

— centre each line of this block of text

UNIT 8

UNIT 9

**REVIEW FUNCTIONS
PROOFREAD A DOCUMENT**

Review of functions

You have now learnt to undertake a number of basic functions and operations on your word processing system. In Assignment 9 you will review and revise these operations to ensure that you are completely familiar with them before you learn more functions. Assignment 9 contains only those functions that you have already covered. If you are unsure about any operation you should refer back to the Method Block of the appropriate unit.

In addition to the operations to be carried out on the word processing system, Assignment 9 requires you to proofread and check the document that appears on page 76. The document contains some spelling and typing errors and these should be corrected when you key in the document. Use your dictionary to check on the spelling of any word about which you are unsure. Identify the errors and mark them with the correction signs shown on page 50.

Key in a correct copy of the document, following the instructions given on the Word Processing Request Form.

ZOCAR WORD AND DATA PROCESSING LIMITED – WORD PROCESSING REQUEST FORM   ASSIGNMENT NO **9**

CREATE a new document ..**✓**..	New document to be named **covers/your initials**
EDIT an existing document	Existing document named ....
LEFT MARGIN AT **22** RIGHT MARGIN AT **78**	Right margin to be – Ragged .... Justified ..**✓**..

LINE SPACING	PITCH	PAPER	NO OF COPIES REQUIRED
1 ..**✓**.. 1½ ..... 2 ..... AND/~~OR~~ as shown on draft ..**✓**..	12 ..**✓**.. 10	Plain A4 ..**✓**.. Headed A4	Print ..**1**.. copy~~(ies)~~

FILING INSTRUCTIONS – RETAIN document on file ..**✓**..   DELETE document from file ......

SPECIAL INSTRUCTIONS

Proofread Assignment 9 before keying in the document.

Identify any errors and mark them with proof correction signs.

Remember to set new ruler lines to change line spacing.

Assignment 9
(Your name)

ZOCAR ACOUSTIC COVERS — *centre*

The Zocar acoustic printer cover is a robust, attractive cver specially designed to reduce noise levels in the modern office. It provides a more pleasant working enviroment for your staff and improves productivity. The cover has many features:

(Double line spacing and centre each line)

Smoked acrylic topin brown or green
Heavy gauge sheet steel casing
Complete visability and access
Ultra-silent fan for air circulation
Fits most matrix and daisy wheel printers
One - year warranty

The Zocar acoustic printer cover is extreemly good value at only only £195 plus £5 delivery, exclusive of VAT. We invite you to try one of our covers absolutely free of charge for 30 days. Your staff will soon convince you that you should order a Zocar cover.

(Centre each line)

ZOCAR ACOUSTIC   COVERS FOR YOUR PRINTERS

ZOCAR WROD AND DATA PROCESSESSING LIMITED
1 Exhibition Square
SOUTHPORT
Merseyside
PR9 2EG

Telephone (0704) 393935

UNIT 10

UNDERLINING TEXT
BOLD TYPE, OR EMBOLDENING

Underlining text

If you wish to underline a heading, phrase or sentence in the text, it is not possible to use the underscore key as you would on a conventional typewriter. A special **underline function** must be used, and this usually involves three steps.

1. The system must first be instructed that a heading or a part of the text is to be underlined.
2. It must then be told how much of the text is to be underlined.
3. A command must be given to execute, or carry out, the underlining operation.

On the majority of word processing systems the underlining operation starts by placing the cursor over the first character of the portion of text to be underlined. The system is then given the instruction to use the underline function. Where dedicated keys are provided this may involve pressing only the CODE plus UNDERLINE keys. If your word processor does not have a dedicated function key for underlining, you may need to press a code key followed by a series of alphabet character keys.

The amount of text to be underlined is then indicated. This may be done by moving the cursor along to the last character of the text to be underlined. On many word processors the system will highlight the text that is being selected for underlining by **reverse video**, which means that the selected text will be shown on the screen with the colours of the characters and the background reversed. This helps the operator to see exactly what is happening and to ensure that the correct amount of text is underlined.

On some systems the operator indicates the amount of text to be underlined by pressing a special function key for word, line, sentence or paragraph. The sequence to be followed to underline three words might, for example, be CODE key, U key (for underline), WORD key, WORD key, WORD key.

When the text to be underlined has been highlighted or indicated in some way, the EXECUTE, or COMMAND or ACTION key is pressed and the operation is carried out by the system.

Some word processors allow the operator to select the underline function *before* typing the text, and the heading or other item will be underlined as it is keyed in to the screen, until the operator presses the UNDERLINE OFF key.

On many word processors it is possible to see the text displayed with the underlining on the screen, as it will appear when it is printed. However, some systems are not able to show the underlining on the screen, and the underlining takes place only when the text is printed out. It may be possible to press a key to view the service codes so that the operator can check whether the underlining function has been carried out. Obviously, it is a great advantage if the operator can see the text displayed on screen as it will be printed.

Some word processing systems offer a choice of methods of underlining, and text may be underlined continuously or under each separate word, and either single or double underlining may be selected.

Emboldening

The word processing operator has several ways of highlighting printed text so that attention may be drawn to important headings or other items in the document. Words may be typed in capitals, in spaced capitals or underlined. Words may also be **emboldened**, which simply means printed in bold type. The printhead strikes twice on each character, the second striking of each character being very slightly to the right of the first strike, so that the character shows up blacker and thicker than the rest of the text.

As with underlining, the system must be instructed that the text is to be emboldened, the amount of text to be emboldened identified and a command given to carry out the instruction. The cursor is generally placed over the first character of the text to be printed in bold type, and the system instructed to embolden text. Some systems may have special dedicated keys for the BOLD function, while others will use code keys followed by an alphabet key.

The amount of text to be emboldened may be identified by highlighting with reverse video, as with underlining, or alternatively the instruction may be given by following a key sequence such as CODE, BOLD, SENTENCE. The EXECUTE, COMMAND or ACTION key is then pressed to instruct the system to carry out the emboldening function.

Many systems are able to display emboldened text on the screen in the form of characters that are brighter or darker than the rest of the text, and it is a great advantage and time-saver for the operator if the text is displayed exactly as it will appear when it is printed out. If you use a system that is not able to display emboldened text on screen, you will have to check whether text is emboldened by viewing the service codes.

In addition to the use of either the emboldening or underlining functions, printed text may be further emphasised by using both bold print and underlining.

ASSIGNMENT NO 10

METHOD	Write in the space provided below a brief note of the method used on your system, and see Page(s) .... of your system manual.
UNDERLINING TEXT BOLD TYPE OR EMBOLDENING TEXT	

ZOCAR WORD AND DATA PROCESSING LIMITED – WORD PROCESSING REQUEST FORM   ASSIGNMENT NO 10

CREATE a new document	New document to be named		
EDIT an existing document ✓	Existing document named *covers/your initials*		
LEFT MARGIN AT ..*22*.. RIGHT MARGIN AT ..*78*..	Right margin to be – Ragged .... Justified ..✓..		
LINE SPACING	PITCH	PAPER	NO OF COPIES REQUIRED
1 ..... 1½ ..... 2 ..... ~~AND~~/OR as shown on draft ..✓..	12 ..✓.. 10	Plain A4 ..✓.. Headed A4	Print ..*1*.. copy~~(ies)~~
FILING INSTRUCTIONS – RETAIN document on file ..✓.. DELETE document from file			
SPECIAL INSTRUCTIONS			

UNIT 10

Assignment 10
(Your name)

ZOCAR ACOUSTIC COVERS [underline]

The **Zocar** acoustic printer cover is a robust, attractive cover specially designed to reduce noise levels in the modern office. It provides a more pleasant working environment for your staff and improves productivity. The cover has many features:

      Smoked acrylic top in brown or green

      Heavy gauge sheet steel casing

      Complete visibility and access

      Ultra-silent fan for air circulation

      Fits most matrix and daisy wheel printers

      One-year warranty

The **Zocar** acoustic printer cover is extremely good value at only £195 plus £5 delivery, exclusive of VAT. We invite you to try one of our covers absolutely free of charge for 30 days. Your staff will soon convince you that you should order a **Zocar** cover.

<u>ZOCAR ACOUSTIC COVERS FOR YOUR PRINTERS</u>

ZOCAR WORD AND DATA PROCESSING LIMITED
1 Exhibition Square
SOUTHPORT
Merseyside
PR9 2EG

<u>Telephone (0704) 393935</u>

UNIT 11

**REMOVE UNDERLINING • REMOVE BOLD TYPE
REMOVE CENTRING**

Remove underline

When a draft has been printed out, the author may decide to make a change in the text and may ask for the underlining to be removed from a heading or from other items. Alternatively, the operator may find during the proofreading stage that words in the text have been underlined incorrectly, and may need to remove the underline instruction.

The cursor is generally placed on the first character of the section from which underlining is to be removed. The amount of text from which the underline is to be removed is then indicated, and the EXECUTE command given. The word processing system will remove the underlining.

If the system displays text on screen as it will be printed, the operator can see immediately that the function has been carried out because the underlining disappears from the screen. Where the underlining does not appear on the screen display, it is necessary to check the service codes to ensure that the operation has been carried out correctly. This type of operation clearly demonstrates the advantages, both in operator confidence and in time saved, of systems that show text on the screen as it will be printed out.

Remove bold type

The instruction to embolden text may be removed in a similar way. The system is given an instruction to remove bold type, the quantity of text from which the bold type is to be removed is identified and the EXECUTE command is given so that the operation is carried out.

If the word processor does not display emboldened text on the screen, it is necessary for the operator to check the service codes to ensure that the operation has been carried out accurately.

Remove centring

Centring commands may also be removed, if desired. The system is instructed to remove centring or delete centring from the required portion of text, and the EXECUTE key pressed so that the operation is carried out. Text that has been displayed as centred on the screen will be moved back to the left margin of the document.

ASSIGNMENT NO 11

METHOD	Write in the space provided below a brief note of the method used on your system, and see Page(s) .... of your system manual.
REMOVE UNDERLINING	
REMOVE BOLD TYPE	
REMOVE CENTRING	

ZOCAR WORD AND DATA PROCESSING LIMITED - WORD PROCESSING REQUEST FORM ASSIGNMENT NO 11

CREATE a new document	New document to be named		
EDIT an existing document ✓	Existing document named *covers/your initials*		
LEFT MARGIN AT ..22.... RIGHT MARGIN AT ..78....	Right margin to be - Ragged .... Justified ✓		
LINE SPACING	PITCH	PAPER	NO OF COPIES REQUIRED
1 ..... 1½ ..... 2 ..... ~~AND~~/OR as shown on draft ✓	12 ✓ 10	Plain A4 ✓ Headed A4	Print ..1.. copy ~~(ies)~~
FILING INSTRUCTIONS - RETAIN document on file ...... DELETE document from file ✓			
SPECIAL INSTRUCTIONS			

Assignment 11
(Your name)

Remove centring →   ZOCAR ACOUSTIC COVERS   *Remove underline*

The **Zocar** acoustic printer cover is a robust, attractive cover specially designed to reduce noise levels in the modern office. It provides a more pleasant working environment for your staff and improves productivity. The cover has many features:

> **Smoked acrylic top in brown or green**
>
> **Heavy gauge sheet steel casing**
>
> **Complete visibility and access**
>
> **Ultra-silent fan for air circulation**
>
> **Fits most matrix and daisy wheel printers**
>
> **One-year warranty**

Remove emboldening and remove centring

The **Zocar** acoustic printer cover is extremely good value at only £195 plus £5 delivery, exclusive of VAT. We invite you to try one of our covers absolutely free of charge for 30 days. Your staff will soon convince you that you should order a **Zocar** cover.

Remove centring from all lines

> ZOCAR ACOUSTIC COVERS FOR YOUR PRINTERS
>
> **ZOCAR WORD AND DATA PROCESSING LIMITED**
> 1 Exhibition Square
> SOUTHPORT
> Merseyside
> PR9 2EG
>
> Telephone (0704) 393935

Remove emboldening

Remove underline

UNIT 12

**LEFT ALIGNED TAB STOP • DECIMAL TAB STOP
RIGHT ALIGNED TAB STOP**

Tab settings

Page formatting, as discussed on page 43, includes the setting of margins, pitch size, line spacing and tabulator stops. On most word processing systems, the tabulator (tab stop) positions are set on the ruler or margin-setting line.

Tab stops can generally only be set *within* the margin settings, i.e., no tab stop can be set to the left of the left margin, or the right of the right margin. The number of tabs that can be set on any ruler line may be limited to 15 or 20 on some systems. However, as several ruler lines may be set on any one page of a document to change margins, new tab positions may be set for a number of headings and columns on a page.

Most systems provide for at least two or three of the following types of tab stop.

Normal or left aligned tab stop	When the tab key is depressed, text will be keyed in from the point at which the tab is set.
Decimal tab stop	When columns of figures that include decimals are to be keyed in, text will appear with all the decimal points aligned under each other.
Right aligned or flush right tab	Text will appear with the last character of each item aligned under the tab position.
Centre tab	Items will be centred under the tab position, thus removing the need to carry out individual centring functions after keying in the text.

Figure U12.1 *Example tab stops*

LEFT ALIGNED OR NORMAL TAB STOP	CENTRED TAB STOP	DECIMAL TAB STOP	RIGHT ALIGNED OR FLUSH RIGHT TAB STOP
All items ranged from the left as shown here	Each item automatically centred as shown here	£123.00 £5,643.20 £4.29 £27,493.50 £27.00	Accounts Dept 29 May Ref JS/WBJ Form 5/a Version 2

An example of each of these types of tab stop is shown in Fig. U12.1. The items have been typed with the same tab stop positions set for the headings and the column items. This clearly shows how items are centred or ranged from the decimal point or from the right.

It would not normally be considered acceptable for the headings to vary in this way. When you are keying in a tabulation containing a mixture of types of tab stop, therefore, it is usually necessary to set one ruler line with 'normal' tabs for the headings, and then to set a new ruler line for the tab positions of the column items.

When the margin-setting line, or ruler, is called up, there is usually a **default** setting of pre-set tab stops already in position. It may be necessary to remove one or more of these tab stops if they are not in the desired position. This may be done in one of several ways, depending on the system being used. A tab stop may be removed, for example, by moving the cursor to the tab stop to be deleted and tapping the space bar.

The tab stop positions are indicated by a symbol or character, for example, 't' for a normal or left aligned tab, 'd' or '.' for a decimal tab, 'r' or 'f' for a right aligned or flush right tab, and 'c' for a centre tab. To set a tab stop, the cursor is moved to the desired position and the appropriate key depressed—for example a 't' for tab or 'd' for decimal tab.

Three separate assignments are provided for this unit to give you experience with normal, decimal and right aligned tab settings. Note that when you are creating a document containing a tabular statement you do *not* use the word wrap facility when you are keying in the table. You must key in a RETURN at the end of each line of the table.

ASSIGNMENT NO 12

METHOD	Write in the space provided below a brief note of the method used on your system, and see Page(s) .... of your system manual.
NORMAL OR LEFT ALIGNED TAB STOP	

ZOCAR WORD AND DATA PROCESSING LIMITED – WORD PROCESSING REQUEST FORM   ASSIGNMENT NO 12

CREATE a new document ✓	New document to be named **tel index/your initials**
EDIT an existing document	Existing document named ....

LEFT MARGIN AT ...**25**......
RIGHT MARGIN AT ...**76**......   Right margin to be – Ragged .... Justified ✓

LINE SPACING	PITCH	PAPER	NO OF COPIES REQUIRED
1 ..... 1½ ..... 2 ✓ AND/OR as shown on draft	12 ✓ 10	Plain A4 ✓ Headed A4	Print **1** copy~~(ies)~~

FILING INSTRUCTIONS – RETAIN document on file ...... DELETE document from file ✓

SPECIAL INSTRUCTIONS

Remember that you will be giving the system instructions to <u>print</u> in double line spacing, and you will <u>not</u>, therefore, need to key in an <u>extra</u> line space between the items in the table.

Your table may appear on the <u>screen</u> in single line spacing, but will be printed out in double line spacing.

Assignment 12
(Your name)

ZOCAR WORD AND DATA PROCESSING LIMITED

[Centre both headings]

TELEPHONE INDEX

[Bold print]

[set left aligned tab stops at 39, 51 and 66]

SURNAME	FORENAME	DEPARTMENT	EXTENSION
ADAMSON	Richard	Buying	74
BRIGGS	Jennifer	Sales	36
CARTER	David	Advertising	49
~~EDWARDS~~	~~Gregory~~	~~Sales~~	~~36~~
HUGHES	Edwin	Marketing	19
KINGSTON	James	Buying	73
KENNINGTON	Anne	Research	22
~~MILWARD~~	~~Olga~~	~~Research~~	~~25~~
LANGLEY	William	Buying	76
MOUNTJOY	Teresa	Sales	39
PRIOR	James	Production	88
WOODLEIGH	Alison	Buying	77

ASSIGNMENT NO 13

METHOD	Write in the space provided below a brief note of the method used on your system, and see Page(s) .... of your system manual.
RIGHT ALIGNED OR FLUSH TAB STOP	

ZOCAR WORD AND DATA PROCESSING LIMITED – WORD PROCESSING REQUEST FORM   ASSIGNMENT NO 13

CREATE a new document ..✓..   New document to be named **sales/your initials**

EDIT an existing document .....   Existing document named ....

LEFT MARGIN AT ...**22**......
RIGHT MARGIN AT ...**79**......   Right margin to be – Ragged ..✓.... Justified ....

LINE SPACING	PITCH	PAPER	NO OF COPIES REQUIRED
1 ..✓.. 1½ ..... 2 ..... AND/~~OR~~ as shown on draft ..✓..	12 ..✓.. 10	Plain A4 ..✓.. Headed A4	Print ..**1**.. copy~~(ies)~~

FILING INSTRUCTIONS – RETAIN document on file ......   DELETE document from file ..✓....

SPECIAL INSTRUCTIONS

Set 2 ruler lines for the tab stops — one for the column headings with left aligned tabs, and a second for the column items with right aligned tab stops.

Type the reference details at the final right aligned tab position.

(Set ruler line here with left aligned tab stops for column heading positions at 43, 54, 63 and 72)

Assignment 13
(Your name)

(Centre each line)

ZOCAR WORD AND DATA PROCESSING LIMITED *(Bold type for this heading)*
Sales Figures — 1 January to 30 June
Magnetic Data Storage Media

ITEM	CENTRAL	NORTH	SOUTH	WALES

(Set a new ruler line here with right aligned tab stops for columns at 50, 59, 68 and 77)

Floppy Disks	123,947	3,509	3,312	1,997
Mini Disks	87,493	2,543	2,277	743
Digital Cassettes	247,651	976	2,784	557
Data Cartridges	9,453	87	874	35
Storage Systems	763	201	95	102
Test Equipment	15	11	5	3
TOTAL	496,322	7,327	9,347	3,437

J Hill
Sales
JH/KAT
July 198_ *(Type in year)*

ASSIGNMENT NO 14

METHOD	Write in the space provided below a brief note of the method used on your system, and see Page(s) .... of your system manual.
DECIMAL TAB STOP	

ZOCAR WORD AND DATA PROCESSING LIMITED – WORD PROCESSING REQUEST FORM   ASSIGNMENT NO 14

CREATE a new document ..✓..	New document to be named ..cables/your initials..		
EDIT an existing document	Existing document named		
LEFT MARGIN AT ...18... RIGHT MARGIN AT ...79...	Right margin to be – Ragged ..✓.. Justified		
LINE SPACING	PITCH	PAPER	NO OF COPIES REQUIRED
1 ..... 1½ ..... 2 ..... ~~AND~~/OR as shown on draft ..✓..	12 ..✓.. 10	Plain A4 ..✓.. Headed A4	Print ...1... copy ~~ies~~
FILING INSTRUCTIONS – RETAIN document on file ...... DELETE document from file ..✓..			
SPECIAL INSTRUCTIONS Set 2 ruler lines for the tab stops — one for the column headings and a second for the column items. Remember that when you have instructed the system to print in double line spacing, the text may appear on the screen in single line spacing — and you should <u>not</u> key in an extra line space after each column item.			

(Set ruler line here for left aligned tab stops for column heading positions at 27, 38, 48, 58 and 70)

Assignment 14
(Your name)

(Centre and embolden heading)

ZOCAR EXTENSION CABLES FOR YOUR WORK STATIONS

	LENGTH (METRES)	PRICE EACH	FOR 5	FOR 10	FOR 20

(Set a new ruler line here with decimal tab stops for column item positions at 29, 42, 52, 64 and 76. Set double line spacing.)

Z0/311	3.05	£15.00	£71.25	£135.00	£260.00
Z0/330	7.6	£20.75	£99.00	£180.00	£349.50
Z0/354	15.2	£23.00	£110.00	£199.75	£390.75
Z0/365	30.5	£31.50	£154.00	£298.50	£579.00
Z0/377	61.0	£65.00	£315.50	£624.75	£1,212.50
Z0/392	91.5	£102.50	£508.75	£1,001.50	£1,198.75

UNIT 13

REVIEW FUNCTIONS
PROOFREAD A DOCUMENT

Review of functions

Assignment 15 helps you to review and revise the functions and operations you have covered in the previous units to ensure that you are completely familiar with these procedures before you learn more functions. The assignment contains only those functions that you have already covered. If you are unsure about any operation, you should refer back to the appropriate unit for guidance.

In addition to the operations to be carried out on the word processing system, Assignment 15 requires you to proofread and check the document that appears on page 94. There are some spelling and typing errors and these should be corrected when you key in the document. Use your dictionary to check on the spelling of any word about which you are unsure. Identify the errors and mark them with the correction signs shown on page 50.

Key in a correct copy of the document, following the instructions given on the Word Processing Request Form.

ZOCAR WORD AND DATA PROCESSING LIMITED - WORD PROCESSING REQUEST FORM   ASSIGNMENT NO 15

CREATE a new document ✓	New document to be named ribbons/your initials
EDIT an existing document	Existing document named .....
LEFT MARGIN AT 15 RIGHT MARGIN AT 79	Right margin to be - Ragged .... Justified ✓

LINE SPACING	PITCH	PAPER	NO OF COPIES REQUIRED
1 ✓ 1½ ..... 2 ..... AND/OR as shown on draft	12 ✓ 10	Plain A4 ✓ Headed A4	Print 1 copy(~~ies~~)

FILING INSTRUCTIONS - RETAIN document on file ✓   DELETE document from file ......

SPECIAL INSTRUCTIONS

Use indented paragraphs as shown. The first line of each indented paragraph begins 5 character spaces in from the left margin. Use the tab key to move the 5 spaces in for the first line of each paragraph.

Remember to RETAIN this document on file, as you will use it for Assignment 16.

Identify any errors and mark them with proof correction signs.

UNIT 13

Assignment 15
(Your name)

[Ruler line here with left aligned tab stop at 20 for paragraph indent]

ZOCAR WORD AND DATA PROCESSING LIMITED
1 Exhibition Square SOUTHPORT
Merseyside PR9 2EG

[Centre each line]

ZOCAR WORD PROCESSOR RIBBONS

[Underline each word]

We stock more than 95 different ribbons, each coded with a production date, so you can be sure of quality and freshness.

Not only do we gaurantee that they will write clearly and legibly, ~~straight from the box,~~ but we can also deliver your order within 24 hours in many parts of the United Kingdom.

u.c. Our quality control group makes sure that each ribbibbon is worthy to bear our name. Only the best is good enough for for us - and you!

Fabrics for nylon ribbons are woven in a precice thread count, but are loosely twisted to withstand your printer's repeated pounding.

Our carbon film ribbons have a longer life than any other carbon film ribbons on the market at at a comparable price. They last for 150,000 characters.

Each ribbon is formulated with the exact percentage of ink required for your printer, and proper control of the ribbon dimensions ensures accurate fit and tracking.

Each ZOCAR ribbon is precision-cut and heat - sealed to prevent fraying. The result is a crisp, clean document that increases your proffessional image.

[Ruler line here with left aligned tab stops at 34, 43, 51, 60 and 70]

COLOUR	CODE	LENGTH	PER 10	PER 100
Multi-strike Black	ZO-64	90 m	£25.65	£245.00
Single-strike Black	ZO-67	100 m	£40.53	£397.47
Fabric Black	ZO-68	15 m	£55.96	£543.75
Teletype Black	ZO-77	39 m	£105.20	£1,000.00
Zocar Special Black	ZO-99	100 m	£135.40	1,240.75

[Ruler line below headings with - left aligned tabs at 34 and 43 - right aligned tab at 57 - and decimal tabs at 64 and 76]

UNIT 14   CUT AND PASTE TO MOVE TEXT

Moving text

One of the most useful functions a word processing system provides is the facility to move whole sections of text from one position in the document to another. This may be done in one of two ways: by 'cutting out' the text, saving it in memory and pasting it in again, or by moving the text up or down the page. Whichever method is used on a particular system, the operation itself is generally known as **cut and paste**.

The name **cut and paste** is very descriptive, because the process is very similar to the operation of cutting up a page of typescript with a pair of scissors, re-arranging the order of the paragraphs and then pasting them in their new order onto another clean sheet of paper. On the word processor, text that is to be moved is identified and 'cut'. On some systems the cut text is removed from the screen and saved in the system's memory; the cursor is moved to the position where it is to be pasted in again, and the saved text appears on the screen again. On other systems the cut text does not disappear from the screen, but is simply moved up or down the screen, travelling over the existing text until the point is reached where it is to be re-located.

On systems that delete the cut text from the screen and save it in memory, it may be necessary to identify a **save area**. In other words, the operator must give the system a name or number for the part of the memory where the saved text is to be stored. This may be called a **save area**, a **putaside area** or a **buffer memory**, and there may be a number of save areas that the operator can use. On this type of system, when the saved text is being recalled for pasting, it must be recalled by using the name or number given to it, in conjunction with the PASTE key.

Depending on the type of system, the contents of the save or putaside area, or the buffer memory, may be retained in the memory until deleted or may be lost when the system is switched off.

The cut and paste function may be used for moving paragraphs or portions of text from one part of a document to another, or even from one document to another completely different document. Although it may be used with small portions of text, this function is most useful when making large changes to a document. Not only does the ability to move text around the document save the time that might otherwise be spent in re-keying the text, but the operator knows that (provided the original text was accurate) the re-located text will be error-free.

Cut and paste to move text

As with all functions, the process is carried out by following a coded key sequence, and where the system is provided with dedicated keys for the cut and paste functions the operation is very simple.

The process of moving text about a document by the cut and paste method is usually carried out in five main stages: (1) identify text to be moved, (2) cut, (3) save, (4) move to new position and (5) paste.

The cursor is positioned at the start of the section which is to be cut. The operator identifies the amount of text to be cut—a word, sentence, paragraph, etc.—usually by moving the cursor to the last character of the portion of text to be cut. The selected text may be highlighted with reverse video or blinking cursors, and this gives the operator the opportunity to check that the correct text is being cut. The operator then presses a key (or keys) to instruct the system to cut the text that has been selected and identified.

On some systems, particularly word processing programs used on microcomputers, the process of identifying text to be cut or moved is carried out by 'marking out' blocks of text. The cursor is moved to the start of the section to be cut and a marker symbol inserted by pressing a particular sequence of keys. A similar marker is inserted at the end of the portion of text to be cut, and the system is instructed to cut, or move, the text between the marker symbols.

On many systems the selected text will then disappear from the screen display. However, it has not been completely deleted, but is retained—or saved—in the system's memory until the operator is ready to recall it. The cursor is moved to the new position at which the text is to be pasted in. The operator then presses the appropriate key or keys and the saved text will be pasted in at the new position.

On other systems the highlighted text is not removed from the screen, but is travelled over existing text to its new position, where it is inserted, the remaining text being pushed down the screen to accommodate it.

Until you are experienced in the use of this function, it may be necessary to check that the correct line spacing has been included both before and after the newly pasted section. If your screen display does not show text exactly as it will be printed out, you may need to print out a draft copy to check your line spacing, and if necessary recall the document to the screen for adjustment of the line spacing before printing out your final copy.

ASSIGNMENT NO 16

METHOD	Write in the space provided below a brief note of the method used on your system, and see Page(s) .... of your system manual.
CUT AND PASTE TO MOVE TEXT	

ZOCAR WORD AND DATA PROCESSING LIMITED – WORD PROCESSING REQUEST FORM   ASSIGNMENT NO 16

CREATE a new document	New document to be named		
EDIT an existing document ..✓..	Existing document named *ribbons/your initials*		
LEFT MARGIN AT ..15........ RIGHT MARGIN AT ..79........	Right margin to be – Ragged .... Justified ..✓....		
LINE SPACING	PITCH	PAPER	NO OF COPIES REQUIRED
1 ..... 1½ ..... 2 ..... ~~AND~~/OR as shown on draft ..✓..	12 ..✓.. 10	Plain A4 ..✓.. Headed A4	Print ...1... copy~~(ies)~~
FILING INSTRUCTIONS – RETAIN document on file ...... DELETE document from file ..✓..			
SPECIAL INSTRUCTIONS *Check the line spacing between paragraphs carefully when you have moved the text with the cut and paste function.*			

UNIT 14

Assignment 16
(Your name)

ZOCAR WORD AND DATA PROCESSING LIMITED
1 Exhibition Square
SOUTHPORT
Merseyside
PR9 2EG

ZOCAR WORD PROCESSOR RIBBONS

We stock more than 95 different ribbons, each coded with a production date, so you can be sure of quality and freshness.

Not only do we guarantee that ZOCAR ribbons will write clearly and legibly, but we can also deliver your order within 24 hours in many parts of the United Kingdom.

Our Quality Control Group makes sure that each ribbon is worthy to bear our name. Only the best is good enough for us - and you!

Fabrics for nylon ribbons are woven in a precise thread count, but are loosely twisted to withstand your printer's repeated pounding.

Our carbon film ribbons have a longer life than any other carbon film ribbons on the market at a comparable price. They last for 150,000 characters.

Each ribbon is formulated with the exact percentage of ink required for your printer, and proper control of the ribbon dimensions ensures accurate fit and tracking.

Each ZOCAR ribbon is precision-cut and heat-sealed to prevent fraying. The result is a crisp, clean document that increases your professional image.

	COLOUR	CODE	LENGTH	PER 10	PER 100
Multi-strike	Black	ZO-64	90 m	£25.65	£245.00
Single-strike	Black	ZO-67	100 m	£40.53	£397.47
Fabric	Black	ZO-68	15 m	£55.96	£543.75
Teletype	Black	ZO-77	39 m	£105.20	£1,000.00
Zocar Special	Black	ZO-99	100 m	£135.40	£1,240.75

UNIT 15

CUT AND PASTE TO REPEAT TEXT
COPYING TEXT • THE UNDERSCORE KEY
REPEAT CHARACTER KEY

Cut and paste to repeat text

In addition to its use in moving items or paragraphs around a document, the cut and paste function is very useful for repeating portions of text, to save the operator the time and effort of repeatedly keying in the same text. In addition, there is the advantage that the pasted text is known to be accurate (as long as the original text was accurate). This use of the cut and paste facility may only be possible if your word processing system is able to save or store the cut text in a save or putaside area, or buffer memory.

There are many applications in which the repetition of text with the cut and paste functions can save time for the operator. The two assignments provided in this section show how it may be used to repeat a form and to insert horizontal lines in a ruled table.

The example in Figs. U15.1 and U15.2 may help to make the operation clear. The operator keys in the basic document, including the text that is to be repeated.

Figure U15.1 *A basic document*

```
ZOCAR WORD AND DATA PROCESSING LIMITED

Daily record of telephone sales calls made

Name ................. Company ............................
Outcome of call ........................................
```

The text which is to be repeated is cut, and pasted in again as many times as the operator wishes to repeat the information. In the example shown, a line space above and below the text would be included in the cut portion. The completed document would then appear as shown in Fig. U15.2.

Figure U15.2 *Repeated text*

```
ZOCAR WORD AND DATA PROCESSING LIMITED

Daily record of telephone sales calls made

Name ................. Company ............................
Outcome of call ........................................

Name ................. Company ............................
Outcome of call ........................................

Name ................. Company ............................
Outcome of call ........................................
```

Copying text

The procedures described above using the cut and paste function to repeat or copy text may alternatively be carried out with the **copy** function. The block of text to be copied is identified, and the cursor is moved to the position at which the copied text is to be inserted. The block of text may be copied several times.

Underscore key

The underline function is used to underline text that has been keyed in. If you wish to key in a horizontal 'ruled' line in the text, you will, on most systems, need to use the underscore key, which is one of the character keys on the QWERTY keyboard. If you are keying in a 'ruled' table, as in Assignment 18, you will need to use the underscore key for the horizontal lines.

REPEAT character key

On many word processor keyboards a REPEAT key is provided, which will allow the operator to repeat a character as often as desired. The operator presses the character key required and at the same time holds down the REPEAT character key until the required number of characters have been keyed in to the screen. This repeat character function is time-saving and is useful when keying in, for example, a continuous line of underscores, or a line of full stops to provide a 'dotted line' for a form.

If your word processor has such a key, you should practise using it in the assignments when you are keying in a line of underscores or full stops.

ASSIGNMENT NO 17

METHOD	Write in the space provided below a brief note of the method used on your system, and see Page(s) .... of your system manual.
CUT AND PASTE TO REPEAT TEXT	
COPYING TEXT	
UNDERSCORE KEY	
REPEAT CHARACTER KEY	

ZOCAR WORD AND DATA PROCESSING LIMITED – WORD PROCESSING REQUEST FORM   ASSIGNMENT NO 17

CREATE a new document ..✓.. New document to be named *parking/your initials*
EDIT an existing document ..... Existing document named ....
LEFT MARGIN AT ....12......   RIGHT MARGIN AT ....79...... Right margin to be – Ragged ..✓... Justified ....

LINE SPACING	PITCH	PAPER	NO OF COPIES REQUIRED
1 ..... 1½ ..✓.. 2 ..... AND/OR as shown on draft	12 ..✓.. 10	Plain A4 ..✓.. Headed A4	Print ...1... copy (ies)

FILING INSTRUCTIONS – RETAIN document on file ...... DELETE document from file ..✓..
SPECIAL INSTRUCTIONS   When you are keying in a form such as this, you must key in a RETURN at the end of each line. Remember to use the REPEAT character key, if your system has one, for the dotted lines.

UNIT 15

Assignment 17

(Your name) *OPERATOR: Press RETURN key only 3 times after your name*

ZOCAR WORD AND DATA PROCESSING LIMITED - VISITOR'S PARKING PERMIT

Date of visit .... Car registration ....
Name of visitor ....
Calling to see ....

OPERATOR: Key in ONE extra line space here

OPERATOR:

Cut, or copy, the text of the document, INCLUDING one line space above ZOCAR WORD AND DATA PROCESSING LIMITED and one line space below the last line of text.

Paste in the text repeatedly, so that it appears 5 times on the completed document.

Remember that although the document will be printed out in 1½ line spacing, it may appear on your screen in single line spacing.

ZOCAR WORD AND DATA PROCESSING LIMITED – WORD PROCESSING REQUEST FORM   ASSIGNMENT NO <u>18</u>

CREATE a new document ✓	New document to be named **disks/your initials**
EDIT an existing document	Existing document named .....

LEFT MARGIN AT **25**
RIGHT MARGIN AT **77**   Right margin to be – Ragged ✓   Justified .....

LINE SPACING	PITCH	PAPER	NO OF COPIES REQUIRED
1 ✓ 1½ ..... 2 ..... AND/~~OR~~ as shown on draft ✓	12 ✓ 10	Plain A4 ✓ Headed A4	Print **1** copy(~~ies~~)

FILING INSTRUCTIONS – RETAIN document on file .....   DELETE document from file ✓

SPECIAL INSTRUCTIONS

Use the cut and paste function, or the copy function to repeat the horizontal lines on the table.

Use the <u>underscore</u> character key for keying in the horizontal line.

Remember to use the REPEAT character key when keying in this line.

UNIT 15

OPERATOR: Set left aligned tabs at 27, 46 and 62

Assignment 18
(Your name)

ZOCAR WORD AND DATA PROCESSING *Centre*

F L O P P Y   D I S K S   *Centre and bold print*

Standard 8" floppy disks

_____

ZFD-1000 Series	Single Sided	Single Density

_____

| ZFD-9000 Series | Single Sided | Single Density |

_____

| ZFD-8000 Series | Single Sided | Double Density |

_____

| ZFD-4000 Series | Double Sided | Single Density |

_____

| ZFD-4000 Series | Double Sided | Double Density |

_____

5¼" minidisks

_____

| ZMD-525 Series | Single Sided | Single Density |

_____

| ZMD-525 Series | Single Sided | Double Density |

_____

| ZMD-550 Series | Double Sided | Double Density |

_____

OPERATOR: Key in this horizontal line, using the underscore character key, followed by a line space (i.e., press RETURN twice).

Copy, or cut and save, the line plus the line space below it.

Paste in the horizontal line after each line of text.

UNIT 16

**PROTECTED SPACE
PRINTING ADDITIONAL COPIES**

Protected space

There are occasions during keying in of a document when the operator may wish to ensure that a group of words or characters is not separated or divided at the end of a line when the system wraps words onto the next line.

It is obviously undesirable, for example, to have names, dates or times divided as shown in Fig. U16.1.

Figure U16.1 *An example of poor line division*

```
        The 'Education and Industry Conference',
sponsored by the Group, was held on Monday, 18
June.  The Conference opened with coffee at 9.00
am in the Reception Room.

        The opening address was given by Mr K G
Satterthwaite, who is the new Chairman of the I &
K Group.
```

On most systems the operator is able to 'protect' the space between characters or groups of words by giving the system a special command, which may involve, for example, pressing a CODE key and the SPACE BAR simultaneously. This will have the effect of providing a character space that is linked to the characters on each side of it, so that the system recognises the whole group as the equivalent of one word when wrapping at the end of a line. The system will usually show a service code symbol to identify the **protected** space. The protected space function may also be used to prevent additional spacing being added during justification.

The name for this function varies from system to system, and it may be called **protected space**, **required space**, **coded space**, **quoted space** or some similar name.

If necessary, the protected space may be removed and this may be done, for example, by the use of the BACKSPACE or DELETE key.

Printing additional copies

Unless it is given other instructions, the word processing system will print out a single copy of each document on any print run. There will be times when you wish to print out more than one copy of a document. When the printing instructions are given to the system, either through a print menu or a print format, the system may be instructed to print out two, three or more copies of a particular document, as required.

Assignment 19 requires you to print out two copies of the document you will key in.

ASSIGNMENT NO 19

METHOD	Write in the space provided below a brief note of the method used on your system, and see Page(s) .... of your system manual.
PROTECTED SPACE PRINT ADDITIONAL COPIES	

ZOCAR WORD AND DATA PROCESSING LIMITED – WORD PROCESSING REQUEST FORM   ASSIGNMENT NO 19

CREATE a new document ..✓.. New document to be named **minutes/your initials**
EDIT an existing document ..... Existing document named ....
LEFT MARGIN AT ..**20**.. RIGHT MARGIN AT ..**79**..   Right margin to be – Ragged ..✓.. Justified ......

LINE SPACING	PITCH	PAPER	NO OF COPIES REQUIRED
1 ..✓.. 1½ ..... 2 ..... AND/OR as shown on draft	12 ..✓.. 10	Plain A4 ..✓.. Headed A4	Print ..**2**.. copy(ies)

FILING INSTRUCTIONS – RETAIN document on file ...... DELETE document from file ..✓..
SPECIAL INSTRUCTIONS Set a left aligned tab stop at 25 for the paragraph indent — and use indented paragraphs. Use 'open punctuation' style, as shown. Remember to print 2 copies.

WORD PROCESSING—SYSTEMS, APPLICATIONS AND ASSIGNMENTS

Assignment 19
(Your name)

[Handwritten note: OPERATOR: Use the 'protected space' function to ensure that NAMES, DATES and TIMES are not 'split' at the ends of lines, as they are on this draft.]

ZOCAR WORD AND DATA PROCESSING [Handwritten: Bold print]

<u>Minutes of meeting
of the Research Department Project Management Team
held at 2 pm in the Committee Room on Wednesday 18 March</u>

PRESENT

   Mr R Andrews (Chairman), Mr R Dean, Mr G Evans, Mr W Le Page, Mr H M Quinn, Ms R J Rowe-Rees, Mr W G Rye, Ms P St John, Ms R J Willis.

APOLOGIES FOR ABSENCE

   Mr D W King, Mrs K L Lee, Mr C V Outhwaite, Mr W G A Rutherford.

MINUTES OF LAST MEETING

   The minutes of the last meeting held on Wednesday 21 January were approved.

MATTERS ARISING FROM THE MINUTES

   Ms Rowe-Rees reported that at the last meeting with G & A Chemicals Limited concerning the new Zopal fluid it had been agreed that two of their staff, Mr W Lever and Miss P Vickery, would visit Zocar Research Laboratories to help with the final trials.

NEW TERMINAL PROJECT

   After lengthy discussion it was agreed that a Project Committee would undertake the management of this project. It was agreed that membership of the Project Committee should consist of Mr Le Page, Mr Quinn, Mr Rye and Ms St John, under the Chairmanship of Mr Evans.

DATE OF NEXT MEETING

   The next meeting was arranged for Wednesday 20 May at 2 pm in the Committee Room.

UNIT 17

OPENING OR MARKING A SPACE
CHANGING THE PITCH, OR SIZE, OF TYPE
CHANGING A PRINTWHEEL
CHANGING A RIBBON

Opening a space for diagrams

It may be necessary on a particular document to leave a specified number of blank line spaces so that a diagram or photograph may be inserted at a later stage. This may be known as **opening** or **marking** a space. Alternatively, the term **protecting a space** may be used for this function instead of for the purpose of protecting character spaces between groups of words as described in Unit 16.

It would, of course, be possible to leave blank line spaces by pressing the space bar for the required number of line spaces and inserting a block of white space in the text. This is what you have been doing so far when typing your assignments, when you wished to leave three or four clear line spaces between your assignment number and name and the start of the assignment. It is, however, more efficient to use the function provided on the word processing system to leave blank line spaces for the following reasons:

1. Anything keyed in to the text, whether it is in the form of words or blank line spaces, takes up space in the memory of the system and on the storage disk. It is desirable to use the space available on a disk as economically as possible. You have already learnt, for example, that double line spacing is set on the format line or ruler line so that text entered in double line spacing appears on the screen, and is stored on the disk, in single line spacing. Lines that are opened or marked with the special function do not occupy space in the memory, except for the single line containing the command.
2. The space that is opened or marked in the text by the use of this function is, on most systems, inserted in single line spacing, regardless of whether the operator has set single, one-and-a-half or double line spacing for the rest of the text. This makes it easier for the operator to be certain of leaving the exact amount of space required.
3. When a document extends to more than one page, the system will regard the opened space as a single unit, and will not break into it to put half on one page and half on the next. Because it has been protected by being marked with special commands, the whole of the opened or marked area will be moved to the following page if there is insufficient room for it on the current page.

The operator follows a very simple procedure for opening a space or marking a space in this way, so that when the document is printed out the required number of blank line spaces are left in the text. A sequence of keys is pressed, for example, a CODE key followed by O (for 'Open'). The system will then ask the operator to state the number of blank single line spaces which are to be opened or marked. The operator keys in the number of spaces required and presses the EXECUTE or COMMAND key. Service codes will indicate to the operator that a space has been marked within the text. Alternatively, an operator prompt may appear on the screen at the opened point in the text which reads, for example, 6 LINES OPENED.

When the document is printed out, the required space will be left within the printed text.

Changing the pitch, or size, of type

On most word processing systems it is possible to print in at least two pitch sizes, the most commonly-used pitch sizes being 10 and 12 pitch. The pitch is the size of type used. With 10 pitch, or Pica type, there are 10 characters to one inch, and with 12 pitch, or Elite type, there are 12 characters to one inch. Some systems provide the facility for 15 pitch type and proportional spacing type to be used. With proportional spacing type, the amount of space given to each character varies depending on the width of the character, the character 'i', for example, being given less space then the character 'w'.

The point at which the instruction is given to the word processing system to print out in a particular pitch size will vary from system to system, but the instruction must be given before the printer is activated. The instruction may be given through a print menu or a print format. Wherever the command is given, it will also be necessary to change the printwheel on the printer, and possibly to change an indicator switch from 12 to 10, or 15.

Changing a printwheel

Care must be taken in handling daisy wheel printheads, or print thimbles. The 'petals' of the wheel are liable to damage if handled roughly, and the wheel should be held carefully by the central raised portion. As the instructions for changing a printwheel vary from printer to printer, you are advised to read the instructions given in the manuacturer's manual.

If you are using a matrix dot printer, there is no printhead to change. Instead, an indicator will be adjusted to alter the size of type.

Assignment 20 requires you to print the document in 10 pitch type.

Changing a ribbon

Changing a ribbon on an impact-type printer (i.e., a daisy wheel, thimble, golfball or dot matrix printer) is simply a matter of removing the cassette ribbon cartridge in use and replacing it with another. The ribbon may be removed because it has been completely used and a new one is required, or you may wish to replace the fabric ribbon with a carbon film ribbon for a particular document. Instructions for changing the ribbon cassette will be found in the manufacturer's manual.

ASSIGNMENT NO 20

METHOD	Write in the space provided below a brief note of the method used on your system, and see Page(s) .... of your system manual.
OPENING OR MARKING A SPACE	
CHANGING PITCH OR TYPE SIZE	
CHANGING A PRINTWHEEL	
CHANGING A RIBBON	

ZOCAR WORD AND DATA PROCESSING LIMITED – WORD PROCESSING REQUEST FORM   ASSIGNMENT NO 20

CREATE a new document ..✓..	New document to be named *binders/your initials*
EDIT an existing document	Existing document named ....

LEFT MARGIN AT ....*12*....
RIGHT MARGIN AT ....*72*....   Right margin to be – Ragged .... Justified ..✓..

LINE SPACING	PITCH	PAPER	NO OF COPIES REQUIRED
1 ..✓.. 1½ ..... 2 ..... AND/OR as shown on draft ..✓..	12 ..... 10 ..✓..	Plain A4 ..✓.. Headed A4	Print ..*2*.. cop*y*(ies)

FILING INSTRUCTIONS – RETAIN document on file ...... DELETE document from file ..✓..

SPECIAL INSTRUCTIONS

Use a carbon film ribbon for printing, if one is available.

110   WORD PROCESSING—SYSTEMS, APPLICATIONS AND ASSIGNMENTS

Assignment 20
(Your name)

[OPEN A SPACE of 3 single lines here]

[Centre each line] *[Bold print]*

ZOCAR WORD AND DATA PROCESSING LIMITED

STORAGE BINDERS FOR PRINTWHEELS AND THIMBLES

Keep your printwheels and thimbles clean and tidy - and safe

Printwheels and thimbles are expensive items~~, and should be cared for~~. If they are left lying around they will get dirty, lost, or broken. *[run on]* Now you can store your printwheels and thimbles in light-weight, compact ZOCAR binders, slim enough to slide into a desk drawer or neatly stack on a book-shelf or desk top.

THE ZOCAR DAISY PARK - ZOB 2343

[OPEN A SPACE of 7 lines here for a photograph to be inserted later]

The ZOCAR Daisy Park holds 6 printwheels. It is compact and secure, even if it is accidentally dropped. Protect your valuable daisy wheels for only £11.50.

THE ZOCAR THIMBLE HOLDER - ZOB 2435

[OPEN A SPACE of 8 single lines here for a photograph to be inserted later]

The ZOCAR Thimble Holder holds 6 thimbles. The sturdy casing protects your thimbles against damage or spillage, yet the contents are easily accessible. Keep your print thimbles secure for only £12.00.

[Left aligned tabs here at 33 and 48 for column headings]

	DAISY PARK	THIMBLE HOLDER
Length	24.77 cm	19.05 cm
Width	29.21 cm	26.04 cm
Depth	1.91 cm	3.49 cm
Weight	0.68 kg	0.45 kg

[Left aligned tab at 22, and decimal tabs at 35 and 50 for column items]

UNIT 18

**REVIEW FUNCTIONS
PROOFREAD A DOCUMENT**

Review of functions

Assignment 21 helps you to review and revise the functions you have covered in the previous units. Remember to proofread and check the document, correcting spelling and typing errors. Identify the errors, marking them with the correction signs shown on page 50, and key in a correct copy of the document following the instructions given on the Word Processing Request Form.

ZOCAR WORD AND DATA PROCESSING LIMITED – WORD PROCESSING REQUEST FORM   ASSIGNMENT NO 21

CREATE a new document ✓	New document to be named offer/your initials
EDIT an existing document	Existing document named .....
LEFT MARGIN AT ...15... RIGHT MARGIN AT ...72...	Right margin to be – Ragged .... Justified ✓

LINE SPACING	PITCH	PAPER	NO OF COPIES REQUIRED
1 ✓ 1½ ..... 2 ..... AND/OR as shown on draft ✓	12 ..... 10 ✓	Plain A4 ✓ Headed A4	Print ...3... cop/(ies)

FILING INSTRUCTIONS – RETAIN document on file ......   DELETE document from file ✓

SPECIAL INSTRUCTIONS

UNIT 18

> **OPERATOR** Use protected spaces between CALCULATOR CALENDAR CLOCK so that these words will all appear on the same line.

Assignment 21
(Your name)

> OPEN A SPACE of 4 lines here

S P E C I A L   O F F E R

Here's a very SPECIAL OFFER to regular customers! Just complete the form below with the names and addresses of several colleages you think wouldlike to recieve a copy of

l.c. of our new Catalogue. As soon as we recieve orders to the value of £ 100 from one or more of them, ZOCAR will send you a FREE credit card size solar - powered CALCULATOR CALENDER CLOCK, pictured below:

> single line spacing

> OPEN A SPACE of 10 single lines here

It's so easy to get our valuble free gift! Just fill in the form and post it in the enclosed FREEPOST envelope.

Name .... Position ....
Company ....
Address ....

> 1½ line spacing

> **OPERATOR** Cut and paste, or copy, this section so that it appears 4 times on the page. Remember to include a clear line space above and below the block of text to be cut or copied.

UNIT 19

**STANDARD AND VARIABLE INFORMATION
COPYING A DOCUMENT
PRINTING ON HEADED PAPER**

Standard and variable information

A standard letter is an almost complete letter which is sent out to clients or customers in connection with a particular subject. Various details are missing from the master version of the standard letter, and these are later keyed in to a copy of the letter to produce an individually printed, personalised document related to the particular customer. The letter contains what is known as the **standard information**.

The information required to complete the missing details may change from customer to customer. These changing details are known as **variable information**, and may include such items as dates, names, addresses and prices. Spaces are left in the standard letter for the variable information to be inserted to suit the particular recipient.

The operator keys in a master version of the standard part of the letter, together with some kind of symbol or indicator, or a coded signal, to show the points at which variable information is required. The master version is then stored on disk for recall and use when required.

Each standard letter is usually identified by a special name or code number, so that the author is able to specify the particular standard document required. In addition, a printed list or form is generally drawn up for the standard document, on which the author can provide details of the variable information to be inserted at each point.

When a completed version of the standard letter is required, the operator copies the document that contains the master version of the letter, leaving the original file copy of the document stored on the disk. The copied document is recalled to the screen, the variable details are inserted at the appropriate points on this copy of the standard letter, and the indicators or signals are deleted. After printing, the completed version of the personalised letter may be deleted from disk, as it is unnecessary to keep a file copy of each customer's letter. It is sufficient for the company to keep a list of the variable details against each customer's name and address record in a separate file store.

In this way, the original master version of the letter is unchanged, and is ready for re-copying and future re-use.

Copying a document

There are many occasions on which the operator will find it useful to edit, or work on, a copy of a document, so that the original is left unchanged. The standard letter application is a typical instance. If the operator recalled the master version of the standard letter and inserted the variable information on this, the original standard letter would have to be completely re-keyed when it was needed again. By making a copy of the original document on the word processor, the operator can make as many changes as desired to the new copy without altering the original.

A document may be copied by following instructions provided on a menu, or by keying in a sequence of keystrokes. On a dedicated system a document may be copied by, for example, pressing the CODE key, the COPY key, keying in a name for the new document and pressing the EXECUTE key. The document to be copied must be given a new name, because a new document is being created.

Printing on headed paper

When headed paper is used for printing, you will need to ensure that the printing starts at the correct position on the paper. This may be done by turning the paper through the print roller a few extra line spaces, so that, after the normal 'default' one inch top margin has been turned up, the printing will start in the correct position.

However, many systems allow the operator to change the number of line spaces in the top margin, when instructions are being given concerning printing. This may be done through the print menu or a print format. If your system offers this facility, you should adjust the top margin so that it allows for the printed heading.

ASSIGNMENT NO 22

METHOD	Write in the space provided below a brief note of the method used on your system, and see Page(s) .... of your system manual.
COPY A DOCUMENT PRINTING ON HEADED PAPER	

ZOCAR WORD AND DATA PROCESSING LIMITED – WORD PROCESSING REQUEST FORM   ASSIGNMENT NO 22

CREATE a new document ..✓... New document to be named ..sales/152/your initials..............
EDIT an existing document ..... Existing document named ....
LEFT MARGIN AT ...25........ RIGHT MARGIN AT ...79........ Right margin to be – Ragged .... Justified ..✓....

LINE SPACING	PITCH	PAPER	NO OF COPIES REQUIRED
1 ..✓... 1½ ..... 2 ..... AND/OR as shown on draft	12 ..✓... 10	Plain A4 ..... Headed A4 ..✓...	Print ...1... copy(~~ies~~)

FILING INSTRUCTIONS – RETAIN document on file ..✓...   DELETE document from file ......

SPECIAL INSTRUCTIONS

Use headed paper.
Key in the standard letter shown in Assignment 22, and file the document. When you have printed Assignment 22, <u>copy</u> the <u>document</u> to make a new document called
    sales/152/your initials/A
Retain both documents on file.

UNIT 19

Assignment 22
(Your name)

[OPEN A SPACE of 4 lines]

Our ref   EJB/your initials

(1)

(2)

Dear (3)

ZOCAR OFFICE EQUIPMENT

Thank you for your recent enquiry in response to our advertisement in the national press about ZOCAR office equipment. I now have pleasure in enclosing literature describing the ZOCAR (4).

The list price of the ZOCAR (4) is (5), inclusive of VAT, discounts being available for quantities.

Our representative for the (6) area is (7), and he will be contacting you in the near future to discuss any specific requirements you may have in connection with ZOCAR office equipment.

Yours faithfully
ZOCAR WORD AND DATA PROCESSING LIMITED

[OPEN A SPACE OF 6 LINES]

Ellis J Bratherton
National Sales Manager

Enc

UNIT 20

SEARCHING
INSERTING VARIABLE DETAILS IN A STANDARD DOCUMENT

The search function

When you are ready to insert variable information in a document, you could simply read through the text on the screen to find the appropriate point at which a set of details is to be inserted, and then move the cursor to that point by means of the cursor movement keys. The new information could then be keyed in and the number indicating the position at which the details were to be inserted deleted.

An alternative method of finding a particular point in a document and moving the cursor directly to that point is to use the **search** function. This command instructs the system to search for a specified word, or words, or even part of a word in the document. The system will then move the cursor to the first occurrence of the word from the point at which the cursor is resting. This function may also be called **search and display**, because the system searches for a word and displays it, or shows it to the operator, without any other action taking place.

The search function is particularly useful in a very long document, where it would take some time to read through the text to find a particular item. It is a very efficient way of moving the cursor rapidly through a document to a particular point when editing a document, and may at times be a more efficient cursor movement procedure than the cursor movement keys you have so far used.

On most word processors the search can begin at the start of the document, at the point where the cursor is currently resting, or at a specified page. On some word processors it is possible to search backwards from the end of a document as well as forwards.

The way in which the search command sequence is carried out will, of course, vary from system to system. It will often be carried out by a series of **question** prompts from the system, to which the operator must key in an **answer** on the status line. The term **string** is often given to the characters which are to be searched for.

The sequence may follow a procedure like this. The operator presses a dedicated SEARCH key, or alternatively a CODE key followed by the 's' key. The system responds by printing a screen message saying 'Search for what?' to which the operator keys in the string of characters forming the word(s) to be searched for. The system may then ask where the search is to start from—the beginning of the document, or a specified page number. When the appropriate command key is pressed, the system searches for the specified string of characters and moves the cursor directly to the first occurrence of the string. The operator can check that the word found is the one required and can take the appropriate action, inserting or deleting text as necessary. Pressing the appropriate command key will then cause the system to move the cursor directly to the next occurrence of the specified string of characters, stopping each time it finds the string, until all occurrences in the document have been found. The system may then display a screen message saying that there are no more **matches** or occurrences of the string.

It is usually important to ensure that the string of characters to be searched for is exactly specified. The system may be **case sensitive**, which means that it may search only for lower case or upper case characters when these are keyed in. If the operator wishes to find ZOCAR, for example, then asking the system to search for Zocar may not result in a successful search, and the system may state that there are no matches. As another example, if the operator wishes to search for the word 'key', then it will be necessary to specify that the system should search for 'space key space', that is, the word 'key' with a character space on each side of it. If this is not done, the system will identify any word in which the characters 'key' occur, and will stop at such words as 'keying', 'keyboard', 're-keying' or 'turnkey'. This is obviously a waste of the operator's time.

Using the search function to insert variable details in a standard letter

You have made a copy of the master version of the standard letter in Assignment 22 and named it **sales/152/your initials/A**. Use this copied version for Assignment 23A and insert, at the appropriate points, the variable details given in the Request for Standard Correspondence Form shown on page 122.

Use the search function to move the cursor directly to the numbered positions. For example, to insert the date, instruct the word processing system to search for (1). Insert the date, delete the bracketed number, and instruct the system to search for (2). Continue in this way until all the variable details have been inserted. Note that the number (4) occurs twice, and you will need to continue the search after you have inserted the details on the first occasion.

On a simple letter such as this, it is obvious that you could carry out the search fairly quickly by reading through the text. However, you should use the search function for this assignment, so that you will gain experience and know how to use it when you are searching through longer documents in future.

When you have finished inserting the variable details, print out a copy of Assignment 23A, and—when your teacher has assessed and approved it—delete the copied document. Take care *not* to delete the master version of the standard letter, as you will need this for Assignments 23B and 23C and for Assignment 24.

For Assignment 23B, copy the document **sales/152/your initials** again, naming the new document **sales/152/your initials/B**, and repeat the process with the details given in the Request for Standard Correspondence Form provided for Assignment 23B.

Repeat the whole process for Assignment 23C, deleting the amended document, but *retaining* on file the master version of the document filed under **sales/152/your initials**.

ASSIGNMENT NO 23

METHOD	Write in the space provided below a brief note of the method used on your system, and see Page(s) .... of your system manual.
SEARCHING INSERTING VARIABLE DETAILS IN A STANDARD DOCUMENT	

ZOCAR WORD AND DATA PROCESSING LIMITED – WORD PROCESSING REQUEST FORM   ASSIGNMENT NO 23

CREATE a new document   .....   New document to be named ....

EDIT an existing document ..✓..   Existing document named **sales/152/your initials/A**

LEFT MARGIN AT ....**25**.....
RIGHT MARGIN AT ....**79**.....   Right margin to be – Ragged ....   Justified ..✓....

LINE SPACING	PITCH	PAPER	NO OF COPIES REQUIRED
1 ..✓.. 1½ ..... 2 ..... AND/OR as shown on draft	12 ..✓.. 10	Plain A4 ..... Headed A4 ..✓..	Print ..**1**.. copy~~(ies)~~ of each letter

FILING INSTRUCTIONS – RETAIN document on file ......   DELETE document from file ..✓....

SPECIAL INSTRUCTIONS

Use the 'protected space' function to avoid splitting the names of the representatives.

Prepare 3 letters with the details given.

Remember to change the Assignment number each time.

UNIT 20

Assignment 23A

```
ZOCAR WORD AND DATA PROCESSING LIMITED
Request for Standard Correspondence - Letter No  sales/152
  (1)  Today's date
  (2)  Mr K C Wilford, Rochester Machine Tools Limited,
       45 Rochester Way, Liverpool, L17 4KM
  (3)  Mr Wilford
  (4)  4997 DG Text/Graphics Matrix Printer   (5) £2,540
  (6)  Liverpool         (7) Mr Alan Surtees
```

Assignment 23B

```
ZOCAR WORD AND DATA PROCESSING LIMITED
Request for Standard Correspondence - Letter No  sales/152
  (1)  Today's date
  (2)  Ms J A Gill, Office Manager, KLC Transport Limited
       19 Roe Lane, Manchester, M3 4QP
  (3)  Ms Gill
  (4)  22500 Electronic Memory Typewriter  (5) £1,950
  (6)  Manchester        (7) Mr Keith Barraclough
```

Assignment 23C

```
ZOCAR WORD AND DATA PROCESSING LIMITED
Request for Standard Correspondence - Letter No  sales/152
  (1)  Today's date
  (2)  Mr C W Poulton, Purchasing Manager, Acorn Machine
       Tools Limited, 2 Carr Street, Leeds, LS1 4AM
  (3)  Mr Poulton
  (4)  M500 Facsimile System            (5) £4,695
  (6)  Leeds        (7) Mr Arnold Roberts
```

UNIT 21

SEARCH AND REPLACE

Search and replace

The search function is very useful when the operator wishes to find a particular word or words in the text so that an item can be checked, without necessarily making any amendments, or as a means of rapid cursor movement through a document to find an item for editing purposes. It is an appropriate function to use when there is a fairly substantial amount of new text to be inserted at a particular point—for example, the address in the standard letter used in Assignments 23A, B and C, or a whole paragraph of new text.

There are other occasions when the operator wishes to search for a word or words and replace them with text of a fairly limited length. Most of the items in the circular letter used in Assignments 23A, B and C would come into this category. The operator may, as you did in those assignments, search for the required string and then replace the existing word with the new wording by using the basic insertion and deletion of text functions.

However, most word processing systems have a **search and replace** facility which enables the operator to instruct the system to search for a particular string of characters and to replace them with a specified alternative string. The operator gives the command for the system to search for a word or words. This may be through a question and answer sequence as described in Unit 20. The system will be instructed to search, for example, for 'Zocar Ltd', and a screen message may ask the operator 'Replace with what?' The operator then keys in to the status line the string that is to replace the string being searched for. If 'Zocar Ltd' is to be replaced by the full name of the company, the operator will key in 'Zocar Word and Data Processing Limited'.

When the appropriate key is pressed to cause the system to execute the command, the search and replace operation may be conducted in one of two ways. The system may automatically move through the whole document, replacing the specified string of characters with the new text each time it occurs. This takes place very rapidly and without any further action from the operator until the whole of the document has been dealt with.

Alternatively, the system may be instructed to stop at each **match**, that is, each time it finds the word it is searching for, to allow the operator to make the 'replace' decision. This gives the operator the opportunity to ensure that words are not replaced in positions that had not been foreseen. Because the search and replace function is a very powerful one, it is generally safer for the operator to use the 'stop at each match' version of the command, so that replacements may be checked.

This is demonstrated in the changes to be made in Assignment 24 to the standard letter, where the company has decided that all its office equipment will in future bear the name ZOQUIP rather than ZOCAR. You are asked to replace the string ZOCAR with ZOQUIP. If you were to use the automatic search and replace function in which the system makes all changes without asking you to check the matches, you would find that you had changed the name of the company, where it appears after 'Yours faithfully' so that it appeared incorrectly as ZOQUIP WORD AND DATA PROCESSING LIMITED. Such accidental changes might go unnoticed on a very long document. You should therefore bear in mind the need for caution in using the automatic function and should make a practice of using the 'stop at each occurrence' version of the command, so that you can make a decision about replacement.

The search and replace operation may begin at the beginning of the document, at the point at which the cursor is currently resting, or at a specified page. On some systems the operation may begin at the end of the document and work backwards, if the operator so wishes. The word processor may require the search to be exact, as far as capitalisation is concerned, as described in Unit 20.

The maximum number of characters that can be searched for, and the maximum number of characters that may be keyed in for replacement, is usually limited and may be anything from about 20 to 60 or so characters, which means that only fairly small changes may be made.

The term **global search and replace** is often used in connection with this function. This simply means that the system is able to search through a whole document, instead of through just a page of the document at a time, which was what some early word processors were limited to. Any word processor that now has the search and replace function is likely to have global search and replace.

ASSIGNMENT NO 24

METHOD	Write in the space provided below a brief note of the method used on your system, and see Page(s) .... of your system manual.
SEARCH AND REPLACE	

ZOCAR WORD AND DATA PROCESSING LIMITED – WORD PROCESSING REQUEST FORM   ASSIGNMENT NO 24

CREATE a new document ..... New document to be named ....

EDIT an existing document ..✓... Existing document named **sales/152/your initials**

LEFT MARGIN AT **25**
RIGHT MARGIN AT **79**   Right margin to be – Ragged .... Justified ..✓..

LINE SPACING	PITCH	PAPER	NO OF COPIES REQUIRED
1 ..✓.. 1½ ..... 2 ..... AND/OR as shown on draft	12 ..✓.. 10	Plain A4 ..... Headed A4 ..✓..	Print ..**1**.. copy(~~ies~~)

FILING INSTRUCTIONS – RETAIN document on file ...... DELETE document from file ..✓..

SPECIAL INSTRUCTIONS

Use the 'search and replace' function to replace the following items on the master version of the standard letter:

    EJB/your initials   <u>with</u>   KLF/your initials

    Ellis J Brotherton   <u>with</u>   Kenneth L Flynn

    ZOCAR   <u>with</u>   ZOQUIP, <u>except</u> in the name of the company.

UNIT 22

REVIEW OF FUNCTIONS COVERED IN THE COURSE
CERTIFICATE OF COMPETENCE IN WORD PROCESSING

You have now completed your first course in word processing. You have covered over 40 different functions and operations, and worked 24 practical assignments. In addition you have learnt:

- what word processing is and its effects on people and employment;
- what a word processor is, together with its associated equipment and supplies;
- the various different types of word processing system;
- some uses of word processing;
- how a word processing system is used;
- what a word processor can do; and
- health and safety aspects of word processing.

There is one more assignment to be completed. You can produce your own Certificate of Competence in Word Processing by keying in and printing a copy of the certificate shown in Assignment 25.

When this has been completed, your teacher, or the head of your department at school or college, will be able to sign the certificate, and provide you with a valuable record of your achievements, which may be shown to a prospective employer as evidence of your ability to operate a word processing system.

Use the best quality paper you can find to print out your certificate, and, if possible, use a carbon film ribbon, or a new fabric ribbon.

ZOCAR WORD AND DATA PROCESSING LIMITED – WORD PROCESSING REQUEST FORM			ASSIGNMENT NO **25**

CREATE a new document ..✓..	New document to be named **certificate/your initials**
EDIT an existing document	Existing document named ....
LEFT MARGIN AT ...**15**... RIGHT MARGIN AT ...**79**...	Right margin to be – Ragged .... Justified ..✓..

LINE SPACING	PITCH	PAPER	NO OF COPIES REQUIRED
1 ..✓.. 1½ ..... 2 ..... AND/OR as shown on draft	12 ..✓.. 10	Plain A4 ..✓.. Headed A4	Print ..**1**.. copy~~(ies)~~

FILING INSTRUCTIONS – RETAIN document on file ...... DELETE document from file ..✓..

SPECIAL INSTRUCTIONS

Set a tab stop at 20.

Use a carbon film ribbon if one is available, or a new fabric ribbon, and good quality paper.

WORD PROCESSING CERTIFICATE OF COMPETENCE *(Bold print)*

T H I S   I S   T O   C E R T I F Y   T H A T

(Centre your name here in bold print)

has completed the course in Word Processing provided in **WORD PROCESSING - SYSTEMS, APPLICATIONS AND ASSIGNMENTS, by Joyce Stananought,** published by McGraw-Hill Book Company (UK) Limited, which included both theoretical instruction and practical experience.

Total number of hours of 'hands-on' experience - *(Insert here the number of hours of 'hands-on' experience you have had.)*

Make and type of word processing system - *(Insert the type of system)*

Functions and operations covered -

    Start-up and close-down procedures
    Create a document
    Set margins and justify right margin
    File a document, recall and edit a document
    Printing single and multiple copies
    Proofreading and proof correction
    Using the index
    Cursor movement
    Insert and delete text
    Change margins and line spacing
    Paragraphing
    Deleting a document from the file
    Inserting additional rulers in text to change format
    Centring lines of text and centring blocks of text
    Viewing service codes
    Underlining text and emboldening text
    Remove underlining, emboldening and centring
    Tab settings - left aligned, right aligned and decimal
    Cut and paste to move text and to repeat text
    Copying text
    Repeat character key and underscore key
    Protected space
    Opening or marking a space
    Changing the pitch, printwheels and ribbon
    Standard letters with variable information
    Copying a document
    Searching, and search and replace

Signed _____   Position _____

School/College _____

Date _____

Word Processing—Personal Record Log Sheet

Date	Time spent on system	Functions covered

ZOCAR WORD AND DATA PROCESSING LIMITED

1 Exhibition Square Southport Merseyside PR9 2EG

Telephone (0704) 393935   Telex 888050

A fictitious organisation: for use with 'Word Processing - Systems, Applications and Assignments', by Joyce Stananought, McGraw-Hill Book Company (UK) Limited, 1984

INDEX

Note: Practical Unit Functions Shown in Capital Letters

Abbreviations file, 29
Access time, 7
Acoustic hood, 10, 38, 76
ADDITIONAL RULERS IN TEXT, 64
Advanced word processing functions, 28, 31
After-glow, 36
Aims of the book, viii
Anti-static cleaner, 14, 37, 48
Arithmetical functions, 33
Ascenders, 8
Audio signals, 20
Audio-typewriting, 4
Author, 3, 4, 5, 34, 61

Background knowledge, 5
Blank space, 23
Bleeps, 20
Blinking, 22, 96
Boilerplating, 32
Bold print, 27, 78, 81
BOLD TYPE, 77–78
Brightness control, 8, 36
Buffer memory, 95, 99

Calculations, 30
Capitals, 26
Case sensitive, 52, 120
Casual user, 4
Central processing unit, 6, 7, 14, 16, 17, 19
Centring, 17, 18, 26, 67, 71, 81
CENTRING BLOCKS OF TEXT, 71
CENTRING LINES OF TEXT, 67
CERTIFICATE OF COMPETENCE IN WORD PROCESSING, 126, 128
Chair, 37, 38
Change bars, 29
Change markers, 29
Character set, 8
CHECK INDEX, 52
Circular letter, 32, 34, 123
Close down routine, 40
Coded space, 105
Command line, 43
Command sequence, 21
Communicating, 16, 18
Communications, 30, 34, 35
Compatible, 30, 34
Computer, 6, 16, 17, 18
   mainframe, 17, 30
   microcomputer, 11, 16, 17, 30, 40, 96
   minicomputer, 17, 30
Consumable items, 13
Control line, 21
Copy function, 100
Copy holder, 37
COPYING A DOCUMENT, 115–16
COPYING TEXT, 99–100
Corrections, 26, 49, 53
CPU (*see* Central processing unit)
CREATE A NEW DOCUMENT, 43
Create function, 43
Cursor, 20, 24, 27, 52, 96, 119, 123

Cursor, dummy, 21
Cursor control keys, 20, 24
CURSOR MOVEMENT, 52
Cursor movement keys, 20, 27, 52–53, 119, 123
Customer records, 33
Cut and paste, 26, 95–96
CUT AND PASTE TO MOVE TEXT, 95
CUT AND PASTE TO REPEAT TEXT, 99

Data processing, 16
Database, 34
DECIMAL TAB STOP, 84–85
Default setting, 44, 85, 116
Delete function, 17, 53
DELETE TEXT, 52
Deleting, 26, 53
DELETING A DOCUMENT FROM FILE, 60–61
Deletion of document, 25, 60–61, 115
Descenders, 8
Desk, 38
Diagrams and charts, 28
Dictionary, 29
Directional arrows, 52
Directories, 33
Directory, 52
Disk (*see* Storage media)
Disk drive, 6, 9, 16
   dual disk system, 10
   single disk system, 10
Document, 24, 25, 27
Document assembly, 32
Document revision, 29, 32, 34
Double check procedure, 60
Draft function, 43

EDIT A DOCUMENT, 52
Edit function, 52
Electrical safety, 38
Electronic mail, 19, 34
Electronic office, 17
Electronic typewriter, 15, 17, 18
EMBOLDENING, 77–78
Emboldening, 27, 78, 81
End of text marker, 22, 23
English, 4
Environment, 36
Ergonomics, 36
Error message, 21
Eyesight, 37

Facsimile (FAX), 17
Filing a document, 45
Financial documents, 33
Flexibility, 5
Flexible working hours, 4
Flickering, 36
Font, 18
Footers, 28
Footnotes, 28
Format, 21, 27, 43, 84
Format line, 21, 44, 64
Forms, 28, 32
Frustration, 7, 37
Function, 21

Glossary, 29

Handbooks, 33
Hard copy, 7
Hard return, 23, 44
Hard space, 23–24
Hardware, 6
Headers, 28
Health, 37, 38
Health and safety, 36–38
Health problems, 36
Help file, 23
Highlighting, 22
Housekeeping, 24–25, 60
Hyphenating, 27
Hyphens:
  optional, 27
  soft, 27

Indent function, 27, 64
Index, 22, 25, 52
Information, 2, 16, 18, 30, 34
Information cycle, 2–3, 5
Information processing, definition, 2
Information technology, 5
INSERT TEXT, 52
Inset text, 64
Inverse video, 22, 71

Justification, 27
JUSTIFIED RIGHT MARGIN, 60

Key:
  action, 9
  backspace, 105
  code, 9
  command, 9
  control, 9
  cursor control, 23
  cursor movement, 24, 27
  dedicated, 9, 15, 95
  delete, 26, 105
  execute, 9
  function, 9, 15, 16
  help, 23
  paste, 95
  repeat, 100
  return, 9, 23, 25, 44, 85
  search, 119
  underscore, 100
Keyboard, 6, 8, 15, 16, 17, 18, 37, 38
  layout, 8–9
  Maltron, 9
  QWERTY, 8–9, 100
Keying in, 8, 23

LAN, 17
Layout, 21, 43
LEFT ALIGNED TAB STOP, 84–85
Legal documents, 33
Line spacing, 27, 45, 57, 64, 96, 108
LINE SPACING – TO CHANGE, 57, 64
List processing, 34
Log in, 40
Logical thinking, 4

Maintenance, 19
Manual:
  operating, 23
  paragraph, 32
  system, 31, 109
  user, 3, 5
  working procedures, 33

Margin:
  default, 44
  justified, 44, 60
  ragged, 44
  semi-justified, 44
  settings, 21, 44, 64
MARGINS – TO CHANGE, 57, 64
MARGINS – SET LEFT AND RIGHT, 43, 44
MARKING A SPACE, 108–9
Marking blocks of text, 96
Match, 119–20, 123–24
Mathematical functions, 30
Memory, 6, 15, 18, 26, 30, 61, 95, 96, 108
Menu, 21–22
  bypass, 21
  main, 22
  sub-menu, 22
Merging text, 29–30, 32, 34
METHOD BLOCKS, 46, 51, 54, 58, 62, 65, 69, 72, 79, 82, 86, 88, 90, 97, 101, 103, 106, 110, 117, 121, 125
Microcomputer (see Computer)
Microprocessor, 16
Mnemonics, 9
Mode, 21
  insert, 53
  overtype, 53
Moving text, 27, 95–96

Networking, 17, 18
Noise level, 38

OCR, 18
Office procedures, 3, 4
One-off documents, 32
OPENING A SPACE, 108–9
Operator:
  qualities of, 4, 5, 18
  dedicated, 4
Operator aids on screen, 20, 25
Operator instruction line, 20, 44
Operator prompts on screen, 20, 37, 109, 119
Optical character recognition, 18
Originator, 3

Page:
  marker, 24
  numbering, 28
  size, 21
Pagination, 24, 27
  automatic, 27
Paging, 24
Paper handling, 12
PARAGRAPH – TO MAKE A NEW, 57
Paragraph numbering, 28–29
PARAGRAPHS – TO RUN TWO INTO ONE, 57
Personalised letter, 32, 115
Personnel records, 33, 35
Photocopier, 17
Phototypesetting, 30
Phrase storage, 29
Pitch, 27, 109
PITCH, OR SIZE OF TYPE – TO CHANGE, 108–9
Principal, 3
Print menu, 21, 43, 105

Printer, 6, 10–12, 16, 17, 18, 19, 27, 109
    bi-directional, 10
    daisy wheel, 10, 11, 12, 109
    dot matrix, 10, 11, 12, 109
    golfball, 10, 11, 109
    hopper feed, 12
    impact, 10, 109
    ink jet, 12
    laser, 12
    letter quality, 10
    non-impact, 10, 12
    sheet feeder, 12
    thimble, 10, 109
    tractor feed, 12
Printhead, 10, 13, 109
Printing:
    additional copies, 105
    on headed paper, 116
PRINTING A DOCUMENT, 49
PRINTING ADDITIONAL COPIES, 105
PRINTING ON HEADED PAPER, 115–16
PRINTWHEEL – TO CHANGE, 108–9
Problem solving, 5
Program, 6, 7, 9, 16, 26, 37
Programmed key sequences, 30
Progressive documents, 33
Prompt line, 20, 21
Proof correction signs, 49, 50
Proofreading, 3, 4, 49, 92, 112
PROOFREADING AND PROOF
    CORRECTION, 49, 74
Protected space, 105, 108
PROTECTED SPACE, 105
Putaside area, 95, 99

Quoted space, 105

Random access, 12
RECALL A DOCUMENT, 52
Recall function, 52
Records processing, 29, 34
Refresh rate, 36
REMOVE BOLD TYPE, 81
REMOVE CENTRING, 81
REMOVE UNDERLINING, 81
REPEAT CHARACTER KEY, 99–100
Report generation, 33–34
Required space, 105
Response time, 7
Retrieval, 33, 61
Reverse video, 22, 71, 77, 96
REVIEW OF FUNCTIONS, 74, 92, 112,
    126
Review questions, 5, 14, 19, 25, 31, 35, 38
Revision tracking, 29
Ribbon, 10, 13, 18, 109
    carbon film, 18, 109
    continuous loop, 14
    fabric 14, 109
    multi-strike, 14
    single-pass, 13
RIBBON – TO CHANGE, 108–9
RIGHT ALIGNED TAB STOP, 84–85
Ruler line, 21, 27, 44, 64, 84

Safety, 36–38
Save area, 95, 99
Screen, 6, 7, 10, 15, 16, 18, 19, 20, 26, 27,
    34, 36–37
    anti-glare, 8, 37
    colour, 8, 36
    filter, 37
    full page, 7
    size, 7
Scrolling, 7, 8, 24
Search and display, 119
SEARCH AND REPLACE, 123–24
Search and replace function, 29, 123–24
    automatic, 123–24
    global, 29, 124
Search function, 119
SEARCHING, 119–20
Seating, 37
Security copying, 24
Selecting, 30, 32, 33
Selection of a system, 19
Serial access, 12
Service, 19
Service codes, 23, 67–68, 77, 105
Shift working, 4
Soft copy, 7
Software, 6
Sorting, 30, 32, 33, 34
Space bar, 24, 105
Spelling check, 29
Staff, selection, 4
STANDARD AND VARIABLE
    INFORMATION, 115
Standard document, 29
Standard information, 30, 34, 35, 115
Standard letter, 32, 115, 120
Standard paragraphs, 32
Starting-up operation, 40
Stationery:
    continuous, 12
    supplies, 14
Statistical documents, 33
Status line, 20–21, 43, 44
Stocklists, 33
Storage, 6, 15, 16, 19, 24, 32
Storage media, 12–13
    disk, 10, 18, 20, 108
        duplicate, 25
        double density, 12
        floppy, 12, 17, 18
        hard, 12, 13, 16
        reading from, 10
        single density, 12
        space left on, 25
        writing to, 10
    diskettes, 12
    magnetic cards, 12, 13
    magnetic tape cassettes, 12, 13, 18
    minidisks, 12
    system disk, 10, 40
    working disk, 10, 40
Storage units, 14
Storing a document, 45
String, 119–20, 123
Subscript, 29
Superscript, 29
Synthesised speech, 18

Tab rack, 21
Tab settings, 21, 84–85
Tab stop:
    centre, 84
    decimal, 84
    flush right, 84
    left aligned, 84
    normal, 84
    right aligned, 84

Tabulation, 27–28
Teamwork, 5
Technical terms, x
Teletex, 30, 34
Telex, 17, 30
Terminal, 16, 17, 34
   Dumb, 7
   Intelligent, 7, 16
Text, 7, 9, 18, 19, 20, 23, 24
Text editing, 15, 18, 26, 31
Thin window display, 15
Trace codes, 23, 67–68
Trace facility, 29
Trade unions, 36
Training, 3, 19, 40
Typewriting, 4

Underline, 17, 77, 81
Underline function, 77, 81, 100
Underlining, 28
UNDERLINING TEXT, 77–78
UNDERSCORE KEY, 99–100
User, 3
Using a word processing system, 20–25
Using the book, ix

VARIABLE DETAILS IN A STANDARD DOCUMENT – INSERTION OF, 119–20
Variable information, 29, 32, 34, 35, 115, 119, 120

VDT, 7, 14
VDU (*see* Visual display unit)
Video display terminal, 7
Viewdata, 30
Viewing, 24, 67
VIEWING SERVICE CODES, 67
Visual display unit, 7, 8, 14, 15, 16, 17, 18, 20, 34, 36, 37, 38
Vocabulary store, 29
Voice activated equipment, 18
Voice input, 19
Voice recognition, 18

Walk-up basis, 3
Waste-bin, 61
White space, 60
Wide document, 7, 8, 24
Word processing, definition, 2
Word processing centre, 3, 4, 19
Word processor, 6
   dedicated, 15–16, 17, 19, 40
   distributed cluster, 16
   shared facility, 16
   shared logic, 16
   shared resource, 16, 19, 40
   standalone, 10, 15–16, 19
   time sharing, 17
   types of system, 15
Word wrap, 23, 25, 28, 44, 85
Work station, 6, 7, 16, 17, 19, 34, 38
Wraparound, 23, 25, 28, 44, 85